Courtyard
KITCHEN

To my family
past and present

Courtyard KITCHEN

Recipes and growing tips for herbs and potted fruits

Natalie Boog

MURDOCH BOOKS

Contents

Getting started

There's so much pleasure in making a delicious dish from something you grew yourself. I was using a lot of herbs in my cooking, and it began to get very expensive to buy them every time. So - the simple solution - I started growing my own. One by one, the number of pots multiplied and I suddenly found I had lots of different herbs.

As each one came into season, there was often an oversupply. I didn't want to waste these lovely herbs, especially after tending to them so lovingly, but I couldn't find one place to go for recipes that just used basil, or just parsley, for instance. So I started collecting my own recipes and I put together some of my favourites.

I like to cook from scratch and I don't use pre-made meals or readymade bottles of sauce. Cooking from scratch doesn't necessarily take lots of time – most of the recipes in this book are easy to make after work during the week, or there are tips on preparing ahead and freezing. My Special

Tomato Sauce (page 35), for example, can be cooked up in one day on the weekend and, if you make enough, it will last the whole year. I've used it in a number of recipes and I hope you'll find more ways to use it as you cook and experiment with your own dishes.

The recipes in the book are varied – if you only have a bit of one particular herb, you can still cook something. Or if you have too much, you can use up all the excess at once. I've also used herbs multiple times, in lots of different combinations, so you'll see, in the Parsley chapter, for example, a recipe that will also use coriander (cilantro) and basil.

There are recipes here for everyone. You don't need to be a chef to cook from this book and I hope you'll be inspired to plant at least one herb and find a favourite recipe that will be your go-to on a regular basis.

When you care for your herbs, you develop a newfound appreciation for where your food comes from. So often, the simple things in life are the best. A little fresh basil can completely change a pasta dish, or a slice of lemon can bring new life to a piece of fish. Fresh herbs are an instant way to really add flavour and when you have some to cut at your back doorstep, you have a world of flavour at your feet.

Feel free to experiment with what you've got – there are no rights and wrongs. If you like the taste, then it's right!

Cut the flower heads from basil and coriander to prevent them from going to seed too quickly.

Plan your garden

The most important thing, before starting your herb garden, is to check out your proposed growing area. The perfect spot should get morning sun, partly shaded midday sun and protection from the hot afternoon sun in summer. In winter, you want as much sun as you can get, as it's less intense and less hot. You'll also need to protect your plants from frosts in winter.

Rosemary, lemons and thyme will thrive in a place that gets full sun all day; basil, parsley, chillies and strawberries like a sunny spot with a little protection from the fiercest sun; coriander (cilantro) and mint will do better in a slightly shaded position.

I often move my pots of herbs around, depending on the season. Different herbs like different amounts of sun, so no matter what your aspect is like, you should be able to grow something. Even if you don't have an outdoor area, you may still have the perfect sunny windowsill to grow a pot or two.

Pots & potting mix

When it comes to pots or containers, you can be as resourceful and creative as you like, as long as the container has good drainage. I've seen herbs growing in old boots, buckets, even on cake stands. I like to use terracotta pots – they are durable, last a long time and look better with age. However, they do tend to dry out quickly in the summer heat.

I also like to put my pots on garden stands or hang them. Having them higher up keeps slugs and snails off them and also means you can have lots of pots in a small area. You may even want to think about a vertical garden. There are many products on the market now, for hanging or displaying multiple pots, or you can make your own, using a ladder, or plant hangers on a wall, a fence or even your balcony rail. You can also get a hanging pot and hook it over the back of a chair if your space is really limited.

The size of the pot you choose will depend on the size of your growing area and on the herb itself. You can also cultivate a number of herbs together in a single, larger pot. Chilli and rosemary grow really well together, for instance, and parsley will happily share a pot with other herbs that need the same amount of sun and water. Mint, on the other hand, is best left in a pot of its own. It has a tendency to spread and become invasive, so don't plant it in the ground or in a pot with another herb.

When potting your herbs, always put a few pebbles in the bottom of the pot. It helps with drainage and stops the soil running out of the drainage holes.

Always use good quality potting mix, as the soil needs nutrients to feed the plant. For a lemon tree, it's best to buy a potting mix designed especially for citrus trees. Normal garden soil is not suitable for pots. Fill the pot with potting mix, and plant your seedlings.

If you pop a rosemary sprig into a glass of water on a sunny windowsill, it will often grow roots.

Seeds or seedlings?

I usually prefer to buy seedlings already established. However, having said that, I often notice that the pot in which a herb has gone to seed – especially basil, parsley and coriander (cilantro) – will spontaneously sprout seedlings the following year, and these plants seems to be much hardier than bought seedlings. I always let my parsley go to seed naturally in this way and regrow on its own, the following year.

If you're patient and want to try growing plants from seed, give it a go. To start with, you will need to buy packets of seed. Some seeds, such as parsley, like to be soaked first – wet some cotton wool, place the seeds on it and watch them sprout. In no time at all, you'll be picking the herb for your wonderful cooking.

When your herbs have finally gone to seed for the first time, collect as many seeds as you can. Store the edible seeds, such as coriander, in an airtight container, making sure they are completely dry, to prevent mould.

Store the seeds that you are saving for cultivating next year, in a brown paper bag. They will stay dry like this until you are ready to plant them.

Planting & growing

Almost all herbs are best planted in spring or early summer, to give you a long growing and harvesting period through the warmer months. If you live in an area that experiences a cold winter, keep young plants protected from any late cold snaps or plant them later in the season.

Annual herbs, such as sweet basil and coriander (cilantro), if planted in spring, will grow through summer and autumn, then go to seed and die naturally, by winter. In a well-protected area, such as a sunny windowsill, you can extend the growing period of late-planted basil into the following autumn and winter. However, this can be a bit trial-and-error – some years I've had success on my kitchen windowsill and other years, I haven't.

Parsley has a natural life cycle that runs over two years before it sets seed and needs to be replaced.

Chillies, thyme, mint and rosemary will grow happily for several years or, in the case of rosemary, for decades. After a couple of years, it's better to replace your chilli plants with younger ones, as they get woodier and less productive. You should also re-pot your chilli plants each year, replacing the soil, as chillies can suffer from root diseases, and re-potting can help prevent any diseases from taking hold.

If you keep strawberry plants well-watered, adequately fed and re-pot them each year with fresh potting mix, they will fruit well for about three years before they need to be replaced. Strawberry plants send out runners that will eventually start to grow on their own. Let them take root in the new soil of a nearby pot, or cut them off close to the original plant. Suspend the new plant in some water and allow the roots to develop a little, then re-pot elsewhere. If you keep trimming off the runners and replanting them in this way, you can put off buying new plants almost indefinitely.

Lemon trees, of course, can live for many years – even in a pot – if well cared for. Once established, they are easy to look after, but you do need to ensure they have a strong and healthy start. Make sure your tree is positioned well – lemons like a lot of sun. If you are keeping your tree in a pot, remember to make sure it always has adequate water, fertilise it regularly and re-pot every one to two years, using new potting mix.

Watering

Water is crucial for any plant, and plants in pots are particularly susceptible to drying out. Watch your basil – if it needs water, then your other herbs will too, particularly coriander (cilantro), parsley and mint.

Even the hardiest plants need some water. Potted lemon trees, for instance, will become stressed if allowed to dry out completely for any length of time – and a stressed plant is more likely to become sick or be attacked by pests.

Obviously, some plants need more water than others. In my vertical garden, I put the ones that need less water, such as thyme, rosemary and sage, at the top, and the ones that need more water, such as basil, in the middle, and mint – the water lover – always at the bottom. As the water drains through each pot, from top to bottom, the plants lower down will naturally get more water.

In summer, I water my pots every day. In winter, however, you should usually only need to water once or twice a week.

Feeding

Hardier herbs, such as rosemary and thyme, really don't need a great deal of feeding, although if they are in pots, a light dose of organic fertiliser, once a month, will ensure that they are adequately nourished.

Basil, parsley, coriander (cilantro), mint and strawberry plants all love a little liquid organic fertiliser, such as seaweed or fish emulsion, which should be applied once a fortnight (or even weekly, for strawberries).

On the other hand, make sure you don't over-fertilise your chillies, as it will only promote more foliage and not much fruit.

Lemon trees need special citrus fertiliser in spring and autumn. This is most important, not only to keep your tree fruiting, but also to keep it healthy and disease resistant.

Pests & diseases

Most herbs are not too prone to pests and diseases, but they do turn up occasionally. Check your basil and mint often, as caterpillars love them. I pick caterpillars off if I see them, but I don't like to use pesticides. If you feel the need to control an infestation, you can spray with a homemade natural garlic and chilli spray (below).

Citrus can be prone to a number of pests, including aphids, 'stink bugs', leaf miner and fruit fly. You can blast aphids off with a strong jet of water from the hose or rub them off with your fingers, and pick off stink bugs and drop them into soapy water (taking care they do not squirt in your eyes). To control leaf miner, cut off affected leaves and spray the remainder of the plant with pest oil. If you are in a fruit-fly area, talk to your local nursery about how to control them, or look on the internet for homemade traps.

Garlic & Chilli Spray

This spray is effective against aphids, caterpillars and other soft-bodied bugs.

5 garlic cloves, crushed
1 small handful fresh red or green bird's eye chillies, chopped
1 tablespoon vegetable oil
1 tablespoon soap flakes or biodegradable dishwashing liquid

Put the garlic and chillies in a medium saucepan with 1 litre (35 fl oz/4 cups) water and bring to the boil. Remove from the heat, add the oil and soap flakes and stir until the soap flakes dissolve. Set aside until cool, then strain the mixture into a spray bottle. Shake before using and spray both upper and undersides of leaves. Keep any unused solution in the fridge and use within 2 weeks. Be sure to wash your herbs well before using them if you use this spray.

Don't harvest all the larger leaves at the bottom of your basil plant - they are giving the plant its energy.

Excess herbs & storage

By picking or cutting back your herbs regularly, you'll promote more growth, so don't be afraid to cut off more than just a couple of stems at a time for your cooking. There will always be somewhere you can use them.

Wrap fresh herbs in wet paper towel or seal in ziplock bags, and store for a few days in the fridge. You can also stand a bunch of herbs in a glass of water and store at room temperature or in the fridge.

Although fresh herbs do not really freeze very well in their fresh-picked state, you can chop them into ice cube trays – about 1 tablespoon per compartment – then cover with a little water and freeze. Store the frozen cubes in ziplock bags and use in cooked sauces, stocks and casseroles.

Chillies, on the other hand, can be successfully frozen, either chopped or whole, in sealed bags, then thawed for use.

You can also dry your excess herbs, especially the harder-leafed ones, such as thyme and rosemary. String the herbs upside down to dry out naturally, then keep them in an airtight container. Alternatively, you can put sprigs on a baking tray and put them in a turned-off oven or one that is at a very low heat, until they are dry and brittle. Cool, then strip the leaves from their stems before storing.

Sterilising bottles & jars

If you plan to preserve some of your homegrown produce, it's really important to sterilise your bottles and jars properly, so that the contents will last without spoiling.

Wash glass bottles, jars and their lids thoroughly in hot soapy water, rinse well, then stand them on a baking tray (with the lids, if they're metal) and put them into a cold oven. Turn the oven to 130°C (250°F), leave them in the oven for at least 30 minutes, then remove.

Pour boiling water over any plastic lids in a bowl and let them sit for about 5 minutes. Remove them from the water with clean tongs, and let them dry on the same hot tray you pulled out of the oven with the glass jars on it. This will help them dry faster. Neither jars nor lids should have any water on them when you fill them.

Try to synchronise this sterilising process with your cooking, as it's best to pour your hot jam or sauce into a hot jar or bottle – otherwise, the glass containers might crack.

Once you have filled a jar, tighten the lid, turn the jar upside down and leave it to sit on the work surface for about 10 minutes. This will help to create a vacuum seal.

Label the sealed jars and keep them in a cupboard out of sunlight.

Basil

Basil Pesto

Pesto Risotto

Basil Meatball Soup

Special Tomato Sauce

Tomato & Chorizo Risotto

Basil Pizza

Roast Lamb with Stuffing

Seafood Stew

Basil & Parmesan Polenta Chips

Chocolate Basil Cake

A pot of sweet green basil is a lovely thing to have in your courtyard. For me, it is the smell of summer. Some of these recipes use a lot of basil and some only use a little. Just cut what you need, when you need it, even if it's only a leaf or two.

You'll notice, through the growing season, that basil stems will become thicker and almost woody. When they start to look like this, you can cut the growth above that point, leaving the big leaves at the base to keep feeding the plants. This will promote new growth and thicken up the bush. You should also cut off the flower heads, to extend the growing season.

If you have success with sweet basil, you might also like to try growing different varieties, such as the pretty purple-leafed basil, slightly aniseed Thai basil or the milder flavoured, small-leafed bush basil, which has the advantage of growing all year round.

Depending on how you want to use it, basil can be chopped finely or coarsely, or torn. However, basil bruises very easily and when you cut it with a knife, the leaves can darken and look a little unpleasant. While this won't affect the flavour, when you're using basil in salads or pasta, it's a good idea to tear the leaves gently, rather than cut them.

Whenever I have excess basil, I always make pesto. Love it.

Basil Pesto

Pesto is one of my favourite recipes and is a staple in my fridge. It has a multitude of uses - serve it on fresh bread with a slice of tomato and a spoonful of cream cheese, dollop it over pizza, in lasagne or simply stir it through hot fresh pasta with shredded chicken or smoked salmon, for a fast and cheap meal.

Makes about 250 g (9 oz/ 1 cup)

4 large handfuls basil leaves
100 g (3½ oz/⅔ cup) pine nuts, toasted
70 g (2½ oz/⅔ cup) finely grated parmesan cheese
4 garlic cloves, chopped
sea salt and freshly ground black pepper
185 ml (6 fl oz/¾ cup) olive oil

Process all the ingredients, except the olive oil, in a food processor until coarsely chopped. With the motor running, slowly add most of the oil until smooth and well combined.

If you feel you need all the oil, then go ahead, but because I cover the top of the pesto with a thin film of oil every time I use it, to prevent it oxidising, I don't add it all.

Pesto will keep refrigerated in an airtight container for up to 2 weeks.

Pesto Risotto

Risotto is my go-to meal. I really love it, and I don't think it's at all hard or laborious to make. Risotto is a cheap and easy dish when all you have to do is stir through some pesto and, if you like, some shredded chicken.

Serves 4

I litre (35 fl oz/4 cups) chicken or
  vegetable stock
50 g (1¾ oz) butter
I small onion, finely chopped
330 g (11¾ oz/1½ cups) arborio
  rice
80 ml (2½ fl oz/⅓ cup) dry white
  wine
50 g (1¾ oz/½ cup) finely grated
  parmesan cheese
125 g (4½ oz/½ cup) Basil Pesto
  (page 28), or to taste
sea salt and freshly ground black
  pepper

Put the stock in a saucepan and bring to the boil, then reduce the heat to low and keep it at a very gentle simmer.

Meanwhile, melt 30 g (I oz) of the butter in a saucepan over medium–low heat. Add the onion and stir for 5–6 minutes, or until soft. Add the rice and stir to coat, then add the wine and cook for 4 minutes, or until evaporated.

Add 250 ml (9 fl oz/I cup) of the hot stock and stir continuously until absorbed. Continue adding 125 ml (4 fl oz/½ cup) of the stock at a time, allowing each addition to be completely absorbed before adding the next. This should take about 20 minutes, by which time the rice should be *al dente*. Remove from the heat, then stir in the parmesan, pesto and remaining butter and season to taste. Serve immediately.

Risotto is a quick meal, cooked within 30 minutes.

Basil Meatball Soup

I look forward to winter and to making lots of soups. This one takes a little more time to prepare, but is well worth the effort as it really is tasty. I think chickpeas are fantastic, so I use them wherever I can. This recipe is a great one for freezing. It will keep in the freezer for up to three months.

Serves 4

2 tablespoons olive oil, plus extra,
    for pan-frying
1 brown onion, finely chopped
3 garlic cloves, crushed
1 x 400 g (14 oz) tin chickpeas,
    drained and rinsed
750 ml (26 fl oz/3 cups) chicken
    stock
sea salt and freshly ground black
    pepper

MEATBALLS
250 g (9 oz) minced (ground) pork
50 g (1¾ oz) bacon, chopped
100 g (3½ oz/1 cup) finely grated
    parmesan cheese
2 tablespoons finely chopped
    basil
1 egg
2 teaspoons grated lemon zest
plain (all-purpose) flour,
    for dusting

Heat the oil in a frying pan over low heat. Add the onion and garlic and sauté for 5–6 minutes, or until soft. Add the chickpeas, chicken stock and 500 ml (17 fl oz/2 cups) water and simmer for 30 minutes, or until the chickpeas are slightly softened. Blend one-quarter of the soup until smooth, then return to the pan, season to taste and combine well. This helps to thicken the soup.

Meanwhile, to make the meatballs, put all the ingredients, except the flour, in a bowl, season to taste and combine well. Using your hands, roll teaspoons of the mixture into small balls, then dust lightly in flour.

Heat 1 cm (½ inch) olive oil in a frying pan and sauté the meatballs for 5–6 minutes, or until golden all over and cooked through. Remove from the pan, then add to the soup and simmer over low heat for 1–2 minutes. Serve hot.

Special Tomato Sauce

I use this versatile sauce as a pasta base, in spaghetti bolognese, or tossed through pasta on its own, or with roasted eggplant (aubergine) and olives. You can also use it in risotto, by substituting the sauce for half the stock. I buy the tomatoes at the end of summer, when they are at their most flavourful and cheapest.

Makes 4 x 500 ml (17 fl oz/ 2 cup) jars

5 kg (11 lb 3 oz) ripe tomatoes
olive oil, for frying
5 garlic cloves, finely chopped
2 brown onions, finely chopped
60 g (2¼ oz/about ½ bunch) basil,
    leaves picked and chopped
sea salt and freshly ground black
    pepper

It's a good idea to make a large quantity, as it keeps well and will never go to waste.

Using a small knife, score the base of the tomatoes to make a cross, then remove the core. Working in batches, drop the tomatoes into a large saucepan of boiling water for about 30–40 seconds. Remove with a slotted spoon and drop into a bowl of iced water, then drain. Peel the tomatoes and chop coarsely.

Heat enough olive oil in a large saucepan to cover the base. Add the garlic and onion and cook over medium–low heat for 6–8 minutes, or until soft. Add the tomato and basil, season to taste, then reduce the heat to low and cook, stirring occasionally, for 1½–2 hours, or until thick and sauce-like.

Spoon the hot sauce into hot sterilised jars (page 20) and seal. Store in a cool, dark place.

Tomato & Chorizo Risotto

Two of my favourite foods - tomato and chorizo - combine in another very easy risotto. If you don't use the whole quantity of Special Tomato Sauce in this recipe, use the remainder later in the week - on a pizza base perhaps.

Serves 4

500 ml (17 fl oz/2 cups) chicken or vegetable stock
500 ml (17 fl oz/2 cups) Special Tomato Sauce (page 35)
2 chorizo sausages, sliced
30 g (1 oz) butter
1 small brown onion, finely chopped
330 g (11¾ oz/1½ cups) arborio rice
80 ml (2½ fl oz/⅓ cup) dry white wine
50 g (1¾ oz/½ cup) finely grated parmesan cheese
sea salt and freshly ground black pepper
chopped basil, to serve (optional)

Put the stock in a saucepan and keep it at a very gentle simmer. Put the tomato sauce in another saucepan and keep it at a low simmer too.

Meanwhile, sauté chorizo in a saucepan over medium heat for 2–3 minutes, or until golden. Remove from pan and reserve. Melt butter in the same saucepan over medium–low heat. Add onion and stir for 5–6 minutes, or until soft. Add the rice and stir to coat, then add the wine and cook for a few minutes, or until evaporated.

Add 250 ml (9 fl oz/1 cup) of the hot stock and stir continuously until absorbed. Continue adding 125 ml (4 fl oz/½ cup) of the stock at a time, allowing each addition to be absorbed before adding the next. Once all the stock has been added, start adding the hot tomato sauce and continue stirring until the rice is *al dente*. This should take about 20 minutes. Remove from the heat, stir in parmesan and chorizo, season to taste, and sprinkle with extra basil, if desired. Serve immediately.

Basil Pizza

*Makes 3 x 22 cm
(8½ inch) diameter pizzas*

250 ml (9 fl oz/1 cup) warm water
7 g (¼ oz/1 sachet) instant yeast
450 g (1 lb/3 cups) '00' strong
    flour
1 tablespoon caster (superfine)
    sugar
1 teaspoon salt
2 tablespoons olive oil
2 tablespoons finely chopped
    basil

TOPPING
Special Tomato Sauce (page 35)
sliced chorizo
black olives
generous amount of mozzarella
    cheese, grated or sliced
small basil leaves, to serve

*This dough freezes
really well. Wrap
each ball in plastic
wrap to freeze, then
thaw before using.*

Put the warm water in a small bowl, sprinkle over the yeast and allow the mixture to stand for 10 minutes, or until frothy.

Combine the flour, sugar and salt in a large bowl. Add the olive oil, basil and yeast mixture and stir until the dough comes together. Turn out onto a lightly floured work surface and knead for 6–8 minutes, or until smooth and elastic. Put the dough in a lightly oiled bowl, cover with a tea towel (dish towel) and stand in a warm place for 1 hour, or until doubled in size. Once risen, punch down the dough and knead briefly. Return the dough to the bowl, cover and leave to rise for another 30 minutes.

Preheat the oven to 240°C (475°F). Put a pizza stone or two heavy-based baking trays in the oven to preheat.

Once the dough has risen, divide it into thirds and roll out on a lightly floured work surface into 22 cm (8 ½ inch) rounds.

For the topping, put each dough round on a piece of baking paper, then spread with the tomato sauce, sliced chorizo, a few olives and top with mozzarella. Transfer two of the pizzas to the preheated pizza stone or baking trays and bake for 10–15 minutes, or until golden and crisp. Repeat for the third pizza. Scatter with basil leaves to serve.

Roast Lamb with Stuffing

Roast lamb is a lovely dinner to share with family or a group of friends. The beautiful stuffing takes this traditional meal to a whole new level, making it extra special. It's all in the preparation, and then you can relax with your guests while it is cooking.

Serves 6

1.4 kg (3 lb 2 oz) boned and rolled
    leg of lamb
olive oil, for roasting
sea salt and freshly ground black
    pepper

STUFFING
100 g (3½ oz) bacon, finely
    chopped
1 tablespoon finely chopped
    flat-leaf (Italian) parsley
1 large handful basil leaves,
    coarsely chopped
3 garlic cloves, finely chopped
2 tablespoons pine nuts, toasted
60 g (2¼ oz/1 cup) fresh
    breadcrumbs
115 g (4 oz/½ cup) ricotta cheese

Preheat the oven to 200°C (400°F).

For the stuffing, put the bacon in a non-stick frying pan and fry over medium heat until golden. Drain on paper towel and cool.

Put the bacon and remaining ingredients in a bowl, season with salt and pepper and mix until well combined.

Remove the string from the lamb, unroll and lay it flat on a board, fat-side down. Press the stuffing along the centre of the meat. Roll the lamb up to enclose the stuffing and tie the roll with kitchen string at 4 cm (1 ½ inch) intervals.

Put the lamb in a large roasting tin, rub with oil and season with salt and pepper. Roast for 1 hour for medium, or until cooked to your liking. Cover the lamb with foil and leave it to stand for 15 minutes before carving.

Seafood Stew

A great meal for friends and family. I love the look of the mussels and and tomatoey sauce, smothered in fresh herbs. It always reminds me of lunches with friends on warm summer days. All the ingredients can be prepared earlier, then thrown together to cook when your guests arrive.

Serves 4

2 tablespoons olive oil
1 small onion, finely chopped
2 garlic cloves, finely chopped
1 tablespoon chilli flakes (or less, to taste)
185 ml (6 fl oz/¾ cup) dry white wine
1 x 400 g (14 oz) tin diced tomatoes
1 handful basil leaves, coarsely chopped
400 g (14 oz) firm white fish, cut into large chunks
500 g (1 lb 2 oz) mussels, scrubbed and beards removed
sea salt and freshly ground black pepper
1 handful flat-leaf (Italian) parsley leaves, coarsely chopped
crusty bread, to serve

In a heavy-based saucepan with a lid, heat the oil over medium heat. Add the onion, garlic and chilli flakes and cook for 5–6 minutes, or until the onion is soft.

Stir in the wine, tomatoes and basil and bring to the boil. Put the fish into the sauce, making sure it's covered as much as possible, then add the mussels on top. Reduce the heat to a simmer, cover the saucepan with the lid, and cook for a further 8 minutes, gently shaking the pan occasionally, but do not take the lid off.

Remove the lid, discard any unopened mussels, season to taste with salt and pepper, scatter over the parsley and serve with crusty bread.

Basil & Parmesan Polenta Chips

When cooked perfectly, these chips have a lovely crunchy crust. They're delicious on their own as a snack, or served with steak and salad. If I'm cooking polenta to eat with another dish, I make extra with a little basil, and refrigerate it, so I have some ready to go for these yummy chips.

Serves 4 as a side

500 ml (17 fl oz/2 cups) chicken or vegetable stock
190 g (6¾ oz/1 cup) coarse polenta (cornmeal)
80 g (2¾ oz/¾ cup) finely grated parmesan cheese
2 tablespoons finely chopped basil
sea salt and freshly ground black pepper
olive oil spray (optional)

Line a 20 cm (8 inch) square glass or ceramic dish with baking paper.

Put the stock and 500 ml (17 fl oz/2 cups) water in a saucepan and bring to the boil over medium heat. Slowly pour in the polenta, whisking until well combined. Reduce the heat to low and cook, stirring regularly to prevent the polenta catching, for about 20 minutes, or until the mixture is thick and comes away from the side of the pan.

Remove from the heat, add the parmesan and basil, season to taste and combine well. Pour the polenta into the prepared dish, cool, then refrigerate for 2 hours, or until firm.

Cut the polenta into chips and cook on a lightly oiled barbecue hotplate until golden and crisp on all sides. Alternatively, spray the chips with olive oil and bake at 180°C (350°F) for 20 minutes, or until crisp and golden. Serve hot.

Chocolate Basil Cake

I was really keen to experiment with basil and sweet flavours. Everyone who has tried this cake likes it, but they are unsure what the flavour is. When I tell them, they recognise it straight away and are amazed.

Serves 8

220 g (7¾ oz/1 cup) caster (superfine) sugar
4 large handfuls basil leaves
100 g (3½ oz) unsalted butter, melted
40 g (1½ oz/⅓ cup) unsweetened cocoa powder
2 large eggs, at room temperature
½ teaspoon baking powder
¼ teaspoon salt
100 g (3½ oz/⅔ cup) plain (all-purpose) flour
125 ml (4 fl oz/½ cup) hot water

FROSTING
60 g (2¼ oz) unsalted butter, softened
55 g (2 oz/½ cup) unsweetened cocoa powder
80 ml (2½ fl oz/⅓ cup) milk
1 teaspoon natural vanilla extract
435 g (15½ oz/3½ cups) icing (confectioners') sugar, sifted

Preheat the oven to 180°C (350°F). Lightly grease a 20 cm (8 inch) round cake tin and line with baking paper.

Process the sugar and basil in a food processor until the basil is finely chopped.

Put the melted butter, cocoa and basil sugar in a bowl and whisk until well combined. Whisk in eggs, one at a time, until smooth and well combined. Stir in the baking powder and salt, then slowly add the flour and stir until just combined. Add the hot water and stir until just combined. Spoon batter into prepared tin and bake for 25 minutes, or until a skewer inserted into the centre comes out clean. Stand for 5 minutes, then turn out onto a wire rack to cool.

For the frosting, beat the butter and cocoa together using an electric mixer, until light and fluffy. Add the milk and vanilla and combine well. Gradually add the icing sugar and beat until smooth. Spread the frosting over the cooled cake. The cake will keep in an airtight container at room temperature for up to 3 days.

Parsley

Celeriac & Potato Soup

Tabouleh

Parsley Pesto

Parsley, Chilli & Lemon Spaghetti

Salmon with Gremolata

Roast Chicken with Herb Stuffing

Salsa Verde

Lamb & Herb Salad

Herb Pilaf

Turkish Potato Salad

Every home should grow a pot or a patch of parsley. It is so easy to grow and look after and is one of the most versatile of herbs. It grows throughout the year in a sunny spot and can be harvested at any time for garnishing almost any dish - from soups to salads and sandwiches - so you'll always find a use for even the smallest amount. And what's more, it's full of vitamins and minerals - even iron.

There are two types of parsley – flat-leaf (Italian) and curly – and although they look different, they are virtually interchangeable.

Parsley can be used as small sprigs for garnishing, or the leaves can be used whole, coarsely torn or finely chopped, depending on your recipe. And, like coriander, even the stems can be used in stocks and stews, as they are full of delicious flavour.

Pruning parsley for use will help to promote new growth, making the bush longer-lasting and preventing it from going to seed. If you want to cut it right back, you'll have enough to make that famous Middle Eastern parsley salad, tabouleh (page 55). But make sure you leave a few leaves on the bush, or otherwise you'll kill the plant.

Although it's best to harvest parsley as you need it, if you find you've picked too much, you can always stand the excess stems in a glass of water on the kitchen bench, where it will last for several days.

Celeriac & Potato Soup

Serves 4-6

1 whole garlic bulb
olive oil
sea salt and freshly ground black
    pepper
1 leek, pale part only, finely
    chopped
500 g (1 lb 2 oz) celeriac, peeled
    and chopped
2 potatoes, coarsely chopped
1 litre (35 fl oz/4 cups) vegetable
    stock

PARSLEY OIL
1 large handful flat-leaf (Italian)
    parsley leaves
50 ml (1¾ fl oz) olive oil

For the parsley oil, process the parsley leaves and oil in a food processor until blended. Strain the mixture through a fine sieve into a bowl.

Preheat the oven to 180°C (350°C).

Slice off and discard 1 cm (½ inch) from the top of the garlic bulb. Put the garlic, cut side up, on a baking tray, drizzle with olive oil and season with salt and pepper. Roast for 30–40 minutes, or until soft. When cool enough to handle, squeeze out each clove to extract the garlic.

Heat a little oil in a large saucepan, add the leek and sauté until softened. Add the celeriac and potato and cook, stirring, for about 10 minutes. Stir in the roasted garlic and stock, bring to the boil, then reduce the heat and simmer for about 30–40 minutes, or until the vegetables are soft.

Process the soup with a stick blender, until smooth, adding more stock if the soup is too thick. Serve in bowls, drizzled with parsley oil.

Tabouleh

Tabouleh is a great side for most barbecued meats or roast vegies. Some recipes include diced onion or chopped spring onions (scallions), but I prefer this light and refreshing version. The pomegranate seeds burst in your mouth, with a lovely juicy sweetness.

Serves 4

90 g (3¼ oz/½ cup) burghul
   (bulgur)
2 tomatoes, diced
I Lebanese (short) cucumber,
   diced
I30 g (4¾ oz/3 cups) finely
   chopped parsley
15 g (½ oz/½ cup) finely chopped
   mint
I25 ml (4 fl oz/½ cup) lemon juice
I tablespoon olive oil
½ pomegranate, seeds removed
sea salt and freshly ground black
   pepper

Put the burghul and diced tomato in a bowl and mix well. While you're chopping all the other ingredients, the tomato juices will help to soften the burghul.

Add the remaining ingredients to the bowl, season to taste, and stir until well combined.

Tabouleh is best served immediately, once prepared, as it doesn't keep for long in the fridge.

Parsley Pesto

I love all types of pesto and there is always a jar of it in my fridge. This pesto is great to toss through pasta with cooked prawns (shrimp), or to serve with toasted flat bread as a snack. I've also rubbed it over a leg of lamb before roasting it and if you've steamed some potatoes, toss this through for an instant hot potato salad.

*Makes about 250 g
(9 oz/1 cup)*

20 g (¾ oz/1 cup firmly packed)
    flat-leaf (Italian) parsley leaves
115 g (4 oz/1 cup) walnuts, toasted
50 g (1¾ oz/½ cup) finely grated
    parmesan cheese
1 garlic clove, finely chopped
juice and grated zest of ½ lemon
sea salt and freshly ground black
    pepper
125 ml (4 fl oz/½ cup) olive oil

Put all the ingredients, except the olive oil, in a blender and pulse until coarsely chopped.

With the motor running, slowly add the olive oil and process until well combined.

If you pour a thin layer of oil on top, the pesto will keep in the fridge for up to 2 weeks.

Parsley, Chilli & Lemon Spaghetti

I love this pasta dish. It's fresh and simple, easy and quick to cook - with lemon and chilli for zing and garlic breadcrumbs for crunchy texture.

Serves 4

2 garlic cloves, crushed
50 g (1¾ oz) butter
60 g (2¼ oz/1 cup) fresh breadcrumbs
375 g (13 oz) spaghetti
1 fresh red bird's eye chilli, seeded and finely chopped
juice and grated zest of 2 lemons
1 handful flat-leaf (Italian) parsley leaves, finely chopped
sea salt and freshly ground black pepper

Put the garlic and half the butter in a large frying pan over low heat. Once the garlic starts to change colour, add the breadcrumbs and stir until golden and crisp. Remove from the pan, set aside and reserve the pan.

Meanwhile, cook the pasta in a large saucepan of boiling salted water until *al dente*, then drain.

Add the remaining butter to the reserved pan and cook over low heat until melted. Add the chilli and cook for 3–4 minutes, or until soft. Add the drained pasta, lemon juice and zest, parsley and a little of the breadcrumb mixture. Season to taste and toss to combine well. Serve sprinkled with the remaining breadcrumbs.

For a less spicy heat, use a long red chilli instead of the bird's eye.

Salmon with Gremolata

Gremolata - a combination of parsley, garlic and lemon - is a really easy way to make any simply cooked fish special, with not a lot of effort. It can be prepared beforehand, however, the fresher, the better. Gremolata is also the traditional garnish for a classic Osso Bucco (page 132).

Serves 4

2 tablespoons olive oil
4 x 180 g (6½ oz) Atlantic salmon
   fillets, skin on

GREMOLATA
150 g (5½ oz/1 bunch) flat-leaf
   (Italian) parsley, leaves picked
   and finely chopped
2 garlic cloves, crushed
grated zest of 1 lemon

For the gremolata, combine all the ingredients in a small bowl and set aside.

Heat the oil in a large non-stick frying pan over high heat. Cook the salmon, skin side down, for 2 minutes. Turn over and cook the other side for 2 minutes, or until golden.

Scatter the gremolata over each fillet just before serving.

Gremolata is also particularly good when scattered over a barbecued steak.

Roast Chicken with Herb Stuffing

I love to make a roast on Sundays and use the leftovers for lunches over the next few days. My grandmother always did this, and it's a nice reminder of her. Be sure to push the butter between the breast skin and meat to help keep the chook extra juicy while cooking.

Serves 4

1.8 kg (4 lb) whole chicken
20 g (¾ oz) butter, softened
sea salt and freshly ground black
   pepper

HERB STUFFING
3 garlic cloves, finely chopped
1 handful flat-leaf (Italian)
   parsley leaves, coarsely
   chopped
1 tablespoon thyme leaves
grated zest of 1 lemon
60 g (2¼ oz/1 cup) fresh
   breadcrumbs
1 egg, lightly whisked
185 g (6½ oz/1 cup) cooked brown
   rice

Preheat the oven to 200°C (400°F). Lightly grease a large roasting dish.

For the stuffing, put all the ingredients in a bowl and stir until well combined. Season with salt and pepper.

Wash chicken briefly under cold running water, remove the neck and giblets, trim any pockets of fat and pat dry with paper towel. Spoon the stuffing into the cavity of the chicken, tie legs together with kitchen string and tuck wing tips under. Put the chicken in the prepared roasting dish. Gently push your fingers under the breast skin and spread the butter under the skin. Season the chicken well with salt and pepper.

Roast for 1 hour 15 minutes, or until the chicken is tender and the juices run clear when the thigh is pierced with a skewer. Cover with foil and set aside to rest for 15 minutes, before carving and serving.

Salsa Verde

Salsa Verde really livens up a meal and I always feel it makes an ordinary meal special. It's a great companion to barbecued meat or fish, but you could also try tossing it through a salad as a dressing or spooning it over steamed pumpkin (winter squash), potatoes or green beans.

*Makes about 250 g
(9 oz / 1 cup)*

2 garlic cloves
1 tablespoon capers, in brine,
    drained
120 g (4¼ oz/1 bunch) basil, leaves
    picked
2 large handfuls flat-leaf (Italian)
    parsley leaves
1 tablespoon wholegrain mustard
60 ml (2 fl oz/¼ cup) white wine
    vinegar
170 ml (5½ fl oz/⅔ cup) extra
    virgin olive oil
sea salt and freshly ground black
    pepper

Finely chop the garlic, capers and herbs and combine them in a bowl. Add the mustard and vinegar, then slowly stir in the olive oil until you reach a sauce-like consistency.

Balance the flavours with salt, pepper and maybe a little more vinegar to taste, if you think it needs it.

*Feel free to adjust
the variety of herbs
to suit your taste
and what you have
on hand.*

Lamb & Herb Salad

Serves 4

500 g (1 lb 2 oz) lamb backstraps
  or loin fillets
3 teaspoons olive oil, plus extra
  for drizzling
2 teaspoons finely chopped
  rosemary
1 teaspoon thyme leaves
sea salt and freshly ground black
  pepper
150 g (5½ oz) cherry tomatoes
250 g (9 oz) haloumi cheese,
  sliced
2 tablespoons coarsely chopped
  flat-leaf (Italian) parsley leaves
1 small handful coriander
  (cilantro) leaves
1 small handful tarragon leaves
1 tablespoon coarsely torn basil
  leaves
1 tablespoon finely chopped mint
4 handfuls rocket
40 g (1½ oz/¼ cup) pine nuts,
  toasted
1 teaspoon balsamic vinegar

Preheat the oven to 180°C (350°F).

Put lamb in a shallow dish, drizzle with a little oil, add half the rosemary and thyme, season with salt and pepper and toss to combine. Leave to stand for 30 minutes.

Put the tomatoes on a baking tray, drizzle with a little oil and season. Roast for 20 minutes, or until soft but not falling apart. Leave oven on.

Heat an ovenproof frying pan over medium–high heat and sear the lamb on both sides, until just browned. Transfer the pan to the oven and roast the lamb for 10–12 minutes, or until it is cooked to your liking. Allow the lamb to rest for 10 minutes, before slicing it diagonally.

Meanwhile, heat a little oil in a frying pan over medium heat. Fry the haloumi for 30 seconds on each side, or until golden. Remove from the pan and tear into large pieces.

Put all the herbs, including the remaining rosemary and thyme, in a bowl. Add the rocket, pine nuts, roasted tomatoes and haloumi.

Whisk oil and vinegar together and season to taste. Pour the dressing over the salad and toss gently to combine. Divide the salad evenly among four plates, top with the sliced lamb and serve immediately.

Herb Pilaf

Pilaf makes a refreshing side dish - and is a good way to use up any excess herbs you have too. It's a very versatile recipe, in that you can really use whichever herbs you like. Try using mint or basil, instead of the coriander.

Serves 4 as a side

1 tablespoon olive oil
½ teaspoon ground coriander
½ teaspoon ground cumin
200 g (7 oz/1 cup) long-grain
   white rice
25 g (1 oz/½ cup) finely chopped
   flat-leaf (Italian) parsley
2 tablespoons finely chopped
   coriander (cilantro)
120 g (4¼ oz/1 cup) finely chopped
   spring onion
20 g (¾ oz/1 cup loosely packed)
   baby spinach leaves, chopped
sea salt and freshly ground black
   pepper

Heat the oil in a saucepan over low heat. Add the ground coriander and cumin and stir for 30 seconds, or until fragrant. Add the rice and stir until it is well coated with the oil, then add 375 ml (13 fl oz/1½ cups) water. Bring to the boil over medium heat, then reduce the heat to as low as possible, cover with a tight-fitting lid and simmer for 15 minutes. Remove from the heat and stand, without removing the lid, for a further 15 minutes.

Stir through herbs, spring onion and spinach, and season with salt and pepper to taste.

*Pilaf is a delicious
accompaniment to
any kind of curry.*

Turkish Potato Salad

A Turkish friend of mine served this salad at a barbecue and I loved it. The tanginess of the lemon and the beautiful red colour from the paprika are what make it unique.

Serves 4

1 kg (2 lb 4 oz) boiling potatoes, peeled and chopped
125 ml (4 fl oz/½ cup) olive oil
1 tablespoon mild paprika
1 teaspoon ground cumin
2 garlic cloves, crushed
juice of 1 lemon
1 handful flat-leaf (Italian) parsley leaves, coarsely chopped
sea salt and freshly ground black pepper

Cook the potato in boiling salted water until just tender. Drain.

Put the oil and spices in a large frying pan and stir over low heat until fragrant. Add the garlic and cook for another 1–2 minutes, or until soft. Add the warm, boiled potato and toss to coat well. Remove from heat, then stir in lemon juice and parsley and season with salt and pepper. Stand for 20 minutes, to allow the flavours to infuse, then serve at room temperature.

If you chill this salad beforehand, be sure to bring it back to room temperature before serving.

Coriander

Guacamole

Corn Fritters

Korma Curry Paste

Thai Chicken Coleslaw

Pork San Choy Bau

Coriander & Chilli Steaks

Vegie Smash

Couscous with Herbs & Almonds

Thai Green Curry Paste

Beef Skewers with Aromatic Pilaf

*C*oriander (cilantro) is the most versatile of herbs, as you can eat every part of it – leaves, stems, roots and seeds. If you have it growing, you can garnish your dishes with a little at a time and, since coriander is kept at its best by constant pruning, this will make it easier to keep your plant bushy and healthy.

Coriander has a tendency to bolt to seed, especially in warm, sunny weather, but if your plant does this, don't despair. Plant new seedlings, let the old plant die down and collect the seeds. Grind them into a powder, using a mortar and pestle or in a spice grinder, and use the ground coriander for cooking. Some curry recipes also use the seeds whole – just lightly toast them to activate the aromas.

Coriander leaves can be used whole, coarsely torn, or finely chopped. Except when using it as a garnish, I also use the chopped stems as much as possible, since they are soft and full of flavour.

And when your plant is finally at the end of its season, remember to keep the roots. These are full of intense flavour and can be frozen, once you have thoroughly cleaned them. Use the chopped roots in sauces or in any recipes where the coriander is blended to a paste.

Coriander always goes well with chilli and lemons – throw these three ingredients together and you can't go wrong.

Guacamole

An oldie, but a goodie. Served with toasted tortilla wedges or celery sticks, it makes a great healthy afternoon snack, or a tasty nibble with a chilled Mexican beer or glass of wine.

Serves 4-6

2 avocados, coarsely chopped
¼ red onion, finely chopped
1 tomato, finely chopped
1 small handful coriander
    (cilantro) leaves, finely
    chopped
juice of 1 lime
fresh long red or green chilli,
    finely chopped and seeded, to
    taste
sea salt and freshly ground black
    pepper

Mash the avocado in a bowl, then stir in the remaining ingredients and season with salt and pepper. Serve immediately.

If you need to store the guacamole before serving, press plastic wrap onto the surface of the dip before putting it in the fridge.

For a spicy variation, add a good pinch of ground cumin to your guacamole.

Corn Fritters

Fritters are a regular dish on my table, as they are quick to prepare, healthy and vegetarian. Make sure you check the Chilli chapter for my Sweet Chilli Sauce - the perfect accompaniment!

Serves 4

75 g (2¾oz/½ cup) plain
    (all-purpose) flour
2 eggs
4 corn cobs, kernels removed
sea salt and freshly ground black
    pepper
olive oil, for pan-frying
coriander (cilantro) sprigs,
    to serve (optional)

SALSA
I avocado, diced
I tablespoon lemon juice
½ red capsicum (pepper), finely
    chopped
½ red onion, finely chopped
I tablespoon chopped coriander
    (cilantro) leaves
I tablespoon Sweet Chilli Sauce
    (page 178)

For the salsa, put all the ingredients in a bowl, season with salt and pepper and combine well.

Put the flour and eggs in a bowl and whisk until smooth. Add the corn kernels, season with salt and pepper and combine well.

Heat a little oil in a large, non-stick frying pan over medium heat. Fry tablespoons of batter for 2-3 minutes on each side, or until golden and cooked through. Drain on paper towel, then serve topped with a spoonful of salsa and a sprig of coriander, if using.

These fritters are delicious for lunch next day!

Korma Curry Paste

If you have extra coriander and want to use it up, this paste can be made in advance. It's incredibly tasty and you won't want store-bought korma paste ever again. Use it in curries by frying off a couple of tablespoons, adding tomato or coconut milk and meat or vegies of your choice. It also makes a delicious rub for meats before barbecuing.

*Makes about 250 g
(9 oz / 1 cup)*

1 tablespoon cumin seeds
50 g (1¾ oz/⅓ cup) unsalted,
    toasted cashews
60 ml (2 fl oz/¼ cup) tomato
    passata (puréed tomatoes)
1 small handful coriander
    (cilantro) leaves
2 garlic cloves, crushed
2 tablespoons desiccated coconut
1 tablespoon garam masala
3 teaspoons finely grated fresh
    ginger
2 teaspoons ground coriander
2 teaspoons mild paprika
2 teaspoons ground turmeric
60 ml (2 fl oz/¼ cup) vegetable oil

Put the cumin seeds in a small dry frying pan and shake over low heat for 3–4 minutes, or until fragrant. Remove from the heat and cool, then grind finely using a mortar and pestle.

Put the ground cumin seeds in a blender with all the remaining ingredients, except the oil, and process until coarsely chopped. Add the oil and process only until it is still quite chunky (which is how I like it) or process for a bit longer, until a smooth paste forms.

Curry paste will keep, in a jar, in the fridge for up to 4 weeks, or frozen for up to 3 months.

Thai Chicken Coleslaw

Crunchy, salty, sweet and spicy – such a refreshing recipe for summer. All the kids I know love it, but I hold back a little on the chilli for them.

Serves 4

1 skinless chicken breast fillet,
    cooked and shredded
1 small Chinese cabbage (wong
    bok), outer leaves discarded,
    finely shredded
2 carrots, finely grated
1 Lebanese (short) cucumber,
    finely grated
50 g (1¾ oz/⅓ cup) unsalted,
    toasted peanuts, coarsely
    chopped
1 small handful coriander
    (cilantro) sprigs, to serve

DRESSING
125 ml (4 fl oz/½ cup) white
    vinegar
75 g (2¾ oz/⅓ cup) sugar
1 teaspoon salt
2 fresh red bird's eye chillies,
    seeded and finely chopped
juice of ½ lime

For the dressing, combine all the ingredients, except the lime juice, in a saucepan. Stir over low heat until the sugar dissolves, then bring to the boil and remove from the heat. Cool, then stir in the lime juice.

Combine the chicken, cabbage, carrot and cucumber in a bowl. Add the dressing and toss to combine. Serve scattered with the peanuts and coriander sprigs.

I keep a few extra nuts to scatter over the leftovers the next day, for that lovely crunch.

Pork San Choy Bau

A great, quick midweek meal. I love the crunch of the lettuce with the Asian flavours and instead of wrapping the pork mixture in lettuce cups, in the traditional way, I sometimes simply fill a bowl with chopped iceberg lettuce and spoon the pork over the top.

Serves 4

1 tablespoon peanut oil
1 teaspoon sesame oil
1 garlic clove, crushed
1 tablespoon finely grated fresh ginger
500 g (1 lb 2 oz) lean minced (ground) pork
1 red capsicum (pepper), finely chopped
1 x 230 g (8 oz) tin water chestnuts, drained and coarsely chopped
60 ml (2 fl oz/¼ cup) soy sauce
2 tablespoons oyster sauce
2 tablespoons Sweet Chilli Sauce (page 178)
2 tablespoons finely chopped coriander (cilantro) leaves
1 iceberg lettuce, trimmed into cups and rinsed in iced water

Heat the peanut and sesame oils in a wok over medium heat. Add the garlic and ginger and cook for 2 minutes, or until fragrant. Add the pork and cook until brown, breaking up any lumps with the back of a wooden spoon. Add the capsicum, water chestnuts and all the sauces and simmer for 3 minutes, or until the sauce reduces a little.

Remove from heat, add the coriander and toss to combine well. Serve in the lettuce cups.

The cooked pork mixture will keep in the fridge for up to 3 days.

Coriander & Chilli Steaks

If you want to jazz up a barbecue, this dish will do it. It has such a lot of flavour, which makes it look as though you've spent hours in the kitchen.

Serves 2

2 beef steaks of your choice
250 ml (9 fl oz/1 cup) white
   vinegar
165 g (5¾ oz/¾ cup) sugar
1 teaspoon salt
1 fresh long red chilli, seeded and
   finely chopped
1 small handful coriander
   (cilantro) leaves, finely
   chopped

MARINADE
1 tablespoon soy sauce
1 teaspoon sichuan peppercorns,
   coarsely ground
1 tablespoon finely grated fresh
   ginger
1 garlic clove, crushed
80 ml (2½ fl oz/⅓ cup) olive oil

For the marinade, combine all the ingredients in a shallow dish. Add the steaks and turn to coat, then cover and refrigerate for 2–3 hours.

Meanwhile, put the vinegar and sugar in a small saucepan and stir over low heat until the sugar dissolves. Stir in the salt, then remove from the heat and cool. Add the chilli and coriander and set aside until ready to serve.

Cook the steaks on a preheated barbecue until done to your liking. Rest for 5 minutes, then serve drizzled with the dressing.

When marinating, allow plenty of time for the flavours to fully develop.

Vegie Smash

I sometimes make this as a main course for dinner if I'm looking for a meat-free night. I also serve it regularly as a share dish. Everyone loves these crunchy roasted vegies with coriander - there's never any left.

Serves 4 as a side

6 small (about 720 g/1 lb 9½ oz) all-purpose potatoes, peeled and quartered

500 g (1 lb 2 oz) butternut pumpkin (squash), peeled and cut into large chunks

400 g (14 oz) sweet potato, peeled and cut into large chunks

olive oil, for drizzling

sea salt and freshly ground black pepper

1 lemon, quartered

1 small handful coriander (cilantro) leaves

50 g (1¾ oz/½ cup) finely grated parmesan cheese

Preheat the oven to 200°C (400°F).

Steam the potato, pumpkin and sweet potato separately, until they are nearly tender but not falling apart.

Spread the potato, pumpkin and sweet potato evenly in a roasting tin and gently smash. Drizzle with oil, season with salt and pepper and scatter the lemon quarters over the top. Roast the vegies, turning occasionally, for 30 minutes, or until golden and tender.

Arrange the roasted vegetables on a serving platter, scatter over the coriander and parmesan and serve while hot.

Couscous with Herbs & Almonds

Couscous is one of those dishes where you can really let your imagination run wild. If you only have a few sprigs of herbs left in your fridge or in a pot, you can throw them in. Never let your herbs go to waste.

Serves 4 as a side

20 g (¾ oz) butter
190 g (6¾ oz/1 cup) pearl (Israeli) couscous
250 ml (9 fl oz/1 cup) chicken stock
1 large handful coriander (cilantro) leaves, coarsely chopped
1 large handful mint leaves, coarsely chopped
65 g (2½ oz/½ cup) slivered almonds, toasted
sea salt and freshly ground black pepper

Melt the butter in a medium saucepan over medium heat. Add the couscous and stir for a few minutes, until well coated with the butter. Add the stock, bring to the boil, then reduce heat to low and simmer, covered, for 8–10 minutes, or until all the liquid is absorbed and the couscous is tender.

Transfer the couscous to a bowl and fluff it up with a fork until all the grains are separated. Stir through the herbs and almonds and season with salt and pepper.

Feel free to vary the herbs according to what you have on hand.

Thai Green Curry Paste

You can make traditional Thai green curry sauce with this paste by frying it off and adding coconut milk. I also enjoy the simplicity of brushing it on skewers of meat or fish for the barbecue.

*Makes about 130 g
(4³/₄ oz/ ¹/₂ cup)*

½ teaspoon coriander seeds
¼ teaspoon cumin seeds
6 white peppercorns
½ teaspoon shrimp paste
¼ teaspoon ground turmeric
4 coriander (cilantro) roots, well
    rinsed and coarsely chopped
2 lemongrass stalks, white part
    only, coarsely chopped
I teaspoon finely grated fresh
    ginger
I fresh long green chilli, seeded
    and finely chopped
4 fresh small green chillies,
    seeded and finely chopped
4 kaffir lime leaves, finely
    chopped
2 red Asian shallots, coarsely
    chopped
4 garlic cloves, coarsely chopped

Put the coriander, cumin seeds and peppercorns in a small dry frying pan and shake over low heat for 3–4 minutes, or until fragrant. Remove from the heat and cool, then grind finely using a mortar and pestle.

Put the ground spices and all the remaining ingredients in a blender. Add a little water and process until a paste forms. Transfer to an airtight container.

Green curry paste will keep, refrigerated in an airtight container, for up to 2 weeks.

Beef Skewers with Aromatic Pilaf

Curry pastes are a godsend when it comes to adding a flavour hit, which is why I always have a jar or two in the fridge. And although it's better to marinate your meat for a couple of hours, it still tastes great if you only have time to toss it together at the last minute.

Serves 4

800 g (1 lb 12 oz) rump steak, cut
    into 2 cm (¾ inch) pieces
1 quantity Thai Green Curry Paste
    (page 93)
8 bamboo skewers, soaked in cold
    water for 30 minutes

AROMATIC PILAF
1 tablespoon peanut oil
1 fresh long red chilli, seeded and
    finely chopped
2 teaspoons finely grated fresh
    ginger
300 g (10½ oz/1½ cups) jasmine
    rice

Put the meat and curry paste in a bowl and toss to coat well. Thread onto the soaked skewers, then cover and refrigerate for 1–2 hours, or overnight, if time permits.

For the pilaf, heat the oil in a saucepan over medium heat. Add the chilli and ginger and cook, stirring, for 1 minute, or until fragrant. Add the rice and stir until it is coated all over, then add 560 ml (19¼ fl oz/2¼ cups) water and bring to the boil. Cover the pan with a tight-fitting lid, reduce the heat to as low as possible and cook for 15 minutes. Remove the pan from the heat and stand, without removing the lid, for 10 minutes.

While rice is standing, cook the beef skewers on a lightly oiled barbecue plate or chargrill pan for 5–6 minutes, or until cooked to your liking. Serve the beef skewers with the pilaf.

Mint

Spicy Salsa Cups

Mint & Pea Pasta

Mint & Honey Lamb Cutlets

Mint Sauce

Vegetable Couscous with Mint

Mint & Coriander Sauce

Thai Beef Salad

Mint Dressing

Beetroot Sorbet

Mint is quite a hardy plant, and not easily killed, so it's a must in your courtyard herb collection - even if you think you're not a gardener. I have had the same mint bush now for about ten years. Every year, it gets eaten overnight back to the stems by caterpillars, but it always recovers into a lovely thick bush. I just have to remember to cut some off for myself before the caterpillars come back!

Mint is a lovely refreshing herb, used for its delightfully fresh taste in dishes, as well as for a fragrant garnish. I really like the use of mint in drinks, both hot and cold, and I love being able to pick just the amount that I need and have it fresh.

The mint grown for use in cooking is mostly common or garden spearmint, and that's the sort you'll usually find in nurseries, but if you've got the space, why not try a pot of peppermint, apple mint, or even the intriguing chocolate mint, as well?

Like basil, mint can be rubbed in your hands to activate the volatile oils before use and it's lovely to brush by a mint bush on a summer's day and smell the beautiful aroma. Also like basil, a pot of mint growing at your back door or near an outdoor table will help to deter flies.

Spicy Salsa Cups

I love any party food that uses healthy fresh ingredients and these are no exception. The filling can be prepared a little ahead of time, but only fill the cups just before serving so they don't go soggy. I guarantee you won't have any left on your plate!

Serves 4 as a starter

3 tortillas, 18 cm (7 inches)
    diameter
1 avocado, finely diced
1 tablespoon lime juice
1 fresh long red chilli, seeded and
    finely chopped
3 teaspoons finely chopped mint
2 teaspoons finely chopped
    coriander (cilantro) leaves
1 teaspoon finely chopped chives
sea salt and freshly ground black
    pepper

Preheat the oven to 180°C (350°F).

Cut each tortilla into quarters and press each wedge-shaped piece into a lightly greased 12-hole mini muffin tin, trimming edges if desired. Bake for 5 minutes, or until golden, then remove from the oven and set aside to cool.

Combine the remaining ingredients in a bowl and season to taste. Spoon the mixture into the tortilla cups and serve immediately.

You can make the tortilla cups a day in advance and store them in an airtight container.

Mint & Pea Pasta

A lovely light, fresh pasta dish that takes just minutes to prepare and cook. With a few staples in the freezer and pantry, and fresh herbs from your garden, dinner is served - hey presto!

Serves 4

350 g (12 oz) shell pasta
150 g (5½ oz) frozen peas
70 g (2½ oz) butter
2 garlic cloves, crushed
1 small handful mint leaves,
    finely chopped
1 small handful basil leaves,
    finely chopped
juice of ½ lemon
sea salt and freshly ground black
    pepper
50 g (1¾ oz/½ cup) finely grated
    parmesan cheese

Cook the pasta in a large saucepan of boiling salted water until *al dente*. Just before the pasta is ready, add the peas and cook for a further 2 minutes. Drain and return the pasta and peas to the pan.

Melt the butter in a large frying pan, add the garlic and cook over low heat for 1–2 minutes, or until soft. Add the drained pasta and peas and combine well. Remove from the heat, add the herbs and lemon juice and season with salt and pepper. Toss to combine well. Serve, sprinkled with parmesan.

*Use pasta
that the peas
can 'snuggle' inside,
such as shells.*

Mint & Honey Lamb Cutlets

Lamb cutlets are one of my favourite cuts of meat. I like to prepare this in the morning before work. Then all I have to do is cook the cutlets and prepare a side of salad or roast vegies.

Serves 2

2 tablespoons honey
1 tablespoon finely chopped mint
1 tablespoon wholegrain mustard
sea salt and freshly ground black
  pepper
6 lamb cutlets, excess fat
  trimmed

Combine the honey, mint, mustard and salt and pepper to taste in a small bowl. Coat the lamb cutlets in the mixture and stand for 1 hour, or longer, if time permits.

Cook the cutlets quickly on a hot chargrill pan over high heat for 2–3 minutes on each side, or until cooked to your liking. Allow to rest for 2 minutes before serving .

*Lamb and mint
are natural
partners!*

Mint Sauce

A classic mint sauce is the traditional accompaniment to lamb, and the Sunday roast just wouldn't be the same without it - but it's also delicious on grilled (broiled) steak or lamb chops, too.

Makes 250 ml (9 fl oz / 1 cup)

185 ml (6 fl oz/¾ cup) white vinegar
165 g (5¾ oz/¾ cup) caster (superfine) sugar
15 g (½ oz/½ cup) finely chopped mint

Put the vinegar, sugar and a pinch of salt in a small saucepan and stir over low heat until the sugar dissolves. Remove from the heat and stand until cool.

Stir in the chopped mint, then pour into a sterilised jar (page 20) and seal.

Mint sauce will keep, unopened, in a cool, dark place for up to 2 years.

Vegetable Couscous with Mint

One of the great things about couscous is that you can experiment with all your favourite flavours. It is best when cooked and eaten the same day, but a little leftover couscous for lunch the next day is still delicious.

Serves 4 as a side

1 sweet potato, peeled and cut into
    small cubes
olive oil, for drizzling
sea salt and freshly ground black
    pepper
½ head broccoli, cut into florets
190 g (6¾ oz/1 cup) couscous
250 ml (9 fl oz/1 cup) boiling
    chicken stock
40 g (1½ oz/¼ cup) pine nuts,
    toasted
2 large handfuls mint leaves,
    finely chopped
juice of 1 lemon

Preheat the oven to 180°C (350°F). Line a baking tray with baking paper.

Put the sweet potato on the prepared tray, drizzle with a little oil, season with salt and pepper and roast for 20–25 minutes, or until golden and tender.

Meanwhile, steam the broccoli until just tender.

Put the couscous in a heatproof bowl, drizzle with a little oil, then pour over the boiling stock. Cover and stand for 10 minutes, then use a fork to fluff up the grains. Add the sweet potato, broccoli, pine nuts, mint and lemon juice and season to taste. Serve at room temperature.

Mint & Coriander Sauce

A wonderfully zingy sauce that is perfect to serve with barbecued meats or fish, or for brushing over a leg of lamb before roasting. You can also use it to dress green salads or a potato salad.

Makes about 250 ml (9 fl oz/1 cup)

1 lemon
1 garlic clove, finely chopped
2 handfuls coriander (cilantro) leaves, finely chopped
2 handfuls mint leaves, finely chopped
125 ml (4 fl oz/½ cup) olive oil
sea salt and freshly ground black pepper

Zest the lemon, then juice one half of the lemon.

Put the zest, garlic and herbs in a bowl and mix until well combined. Stir in the lemon juice and olive oil and season with salt and pepper.

This sauce will keep in the fridge for up to 1 week.

Thai Beef Salad

If I'm serving this salad to friends, I sometimes arrange it in individual cups or jars, taking care to dress each ingredient carefully. It should be eaten straight away. If you don't have Thai basil, use sweet basil instead.

Serves 4 as a starter

2 tablespoons fish sauce

2 tablespoons lime juice

2 tablespoons grated palm sugar (jaggery)

1 lemongrass stalk, white part only, finely chopped

1 teaspoon finely grated fresh ginger

1 teaspoon sesame oil

500 g (1 lb 2 oz) beef scotch fillet

3 Lebanese (short) cucumbers, halved lengthways, seeded, then cut into sticks

1 fresh long red chilli, seeded and finely chopped

1 handful Thai basil leaves

1 handful mint leaves

1 handful coriander (cilantro) leaves

4 kaffir lime leaves, chopped

40 g (1½ oz/¼ cup) coarsely chopped, unsalted toasted peanuts

lime cheeks, to serve

Combine the fish sauce, lime juice, palm sugar, lemongrass, ginger and sesame oil in a small bowl. Put one-third of the marinade in a large bowl, add the beef and turn to coat well. Cover and marinate for at least 1 hour, or longer, if time permits. Reserve the remaining marinade for the dressing.

Cook the beef on a hot chargrill pan or lightly oiled barbecue plate over high heat for 3–4 minutes on each side for medium-rare, or until cooked to your liking. Remove from heat and stand for 5 minutes. Using a sharp knife, cut across the grain into 1 cm (½ inch) thick slices.

Put all the remaining ingredients, except the peanuts, in a bowl and toss gently to combine or arrange in jars. Transfer the salad to a serving platter, top with the meat, then pour over the reserved marinade, scatter with the peanuts and serve with lime cheeks.

Mint Dressing

Although this dressing is perfect for your usual garden leaf or potato salad, you could also try drizzling it over warm couscous. It stores well in the fridge for up to 2 weeks, but be sure to shake it well before use.

Makes 250 ml
(9 fl oz / 1 cup)

185 ml (6 fl oz/¾ cup) olive oil
2 tablespoons white wine vinegar
½ teaspoon sugar
1 tablespoon wholegrain mustard
1 handful mint leaves, finely
    chopped
sea salt and freshly ground black
    pepper

Put all the ingredients in a jar, season with salt and pepper, seal and shake until emulsified.

This basic vinaigrette can be used with just about any herb.

Beetroot Sorbet

I was really surprised the first time I tried this, but I really love it now and often make it for a special-occasion dessert. Make sure you serve it with the mint - it adds a wonderful burst of freshness.

Makes about 1.5 litres (52 fl oz/6 cups)

330 g (11¾ oz/1½ cups) caster (superfine) sugar
3 small (500 g/1 lb 2 oz) beetroot (beets), scrubbed
chopped mint, to serve

In a medium saucepan combine the sugar with 375 ml (13 fl oz/1½ cups) water and stir over low heat until the sugar dissolves. Bring to the boil, then remove from the heat and stand until cool. Refrigerate until chilled.

Meanwhile, cook the beetroot in lightly salted boiling water for 20–30 minutes, or until tender. Drain and cool, then peel and purée until smooth.

Combine the beetroot purée and chilled sugar syrup, then churn in an ice cream machine, according to the manufacturer's directions.

Alternatively, pour the mixture into a shallow tray and freeze until almost hard. Using a fork, scrape the crystals until fine, then return to the freezer to set completely.

Serve the sorbet scattered with chopped mint.

This sorbet will keep for up to 3 months in the freezer.

Rosemary

Potato & Rosemary Pizza

Rosemary Pesto

Herbed Hamburgers

Rosemary Potato Wedges

Pork with Lemon & Rosemary

Osso Bucco

Marinated Lamb Kebabs

Rosemary Lamb Ragu

Flourless Orange & Rosemary Cake

*I*f you find you don't have a naturally green thumb, or can't keep anything alive in the garden - then rosemary is definitely your plant!

I have multiple rosemary bushes in my garden, both in the ground and in pots. Because it responds quite happily to pruning, you can make it ornamental as well as functional. I have seen rosemary grown as hedging in parterre-style gardens. It looks lovely trimmed in this way.

Once your rosemary bush attains some age, you'll notice the stems will start to look woody. If you cut these woody stems and remove all the leaves, except at one tip, you can use them as skewers when making kebabs. They look wonderful and add a subtle flavour to the cooking meat as well.

If I have picked too much rosemary, I put it in a jar with rock salt, seal it tightly and pop it into a dark cupboard. The herb flavours the salt, which can then be used as a seasoning. You can also pop a few sprigs into white wine vinegar, for a lovely subtle flavour.

When using rosemary, strip the leaves from the stalks and either use them whole or chop them finely. You can also throw whole sprigs into stews or soups, or into the roasting tin when baking meat or vegies – the leaves will fall from the stalks. Remember to remove the stalks before serving.

Potato & Rosemary Pizza

As simple as this recipe is, it is delicious! It took me some time to try potato on pizza, but this is now my favourite pizza. Be sure to buy the nice cheeses to go on top - they really add to the flavour.

Makes 3 x 22 cm (8½ in) diameter pizzas

350 g (12 oz) all-purpose potatoes, peeled and thinly sliced
I quantity Basil Pizza dough (page 38)
I tablespoon rosemary leaves
100 g (3½ oz) pecorino cheese, finely grated
100 g (3½ oz) taleggio cheese, thinly sliced
100 g (3½ oz) prosciutto, torn into pieces
sea salt and freshly ground black pepper
olive oil, for drizzling

Preheat the oven to 240°C (475°F). Put a pizza stone or two heavy-based baking trays in the oven to preheat.

Put the sliced potatoes into a saucepan of lightly salted water, bring to the boil and cook for 1–2 minutes, or until tender but not falling apart. Drain and set aside.

Divide the pizza dough into thirds and roll each piece out into a 22 cm (8½ inch) round. Put each round on a piece of baking paper, cover with a single layer of potato and scatter over the rosemary. Scatter most of the cheese over the top, then add the prosciutto. Scatter with the remaining cheese, season with salt and pepper, then drizzle with a little olive oil.

Transfer two of the pizzas to the pizza stone or baking trays and bake for 10–15 minutes, or until golden and crisp. Bake the remaining pizza in the same way.

Rosemary Pesto

Toss this pesto through pasta, rub it onto a leg of lamb before roasting, or serve it on fresh bread with sliced tomatoes and soft cheese. It's also very tasty stirred through freshly steamed vegies, such as green beans or zucchini (courgettes).

*Makes about 250 g
(9 oz/1 cup)*

4 tablespoons finely chopped
   rosemary
3 large handfuls flat-leaf (Italian)
   parsley leaves
1 garlic clove, finely chopped
50 g (1¾ oz/½ cup) finely grated
   parmesan cheese
60 g (2¼ oz/½ cup) walnuts,
   lightly toasted
125 ml (4½ fl oz/½ cup) olive oil
sea salt and freshly ground black
   pepper

Process all the ingredients, except the oil and seasoning, in a food processor until the mixture is coarsely chopped.

With the motor running, slowly add the oil and process until just combined – it should still be a little chunky. Season with salt and pepper.

To store the pesto, transfer it to a small airtight container, pour a little oil over the top and keep it in the fridge.

Pesto will keep in the fridge in an airtight container for up to 2 weeks.

Herbed Hamburgers

There really is nothing nicer than a homemade hamburger with some crispy wedges on the side. I like that I can add whatever I like - my Tomato Relish is a must - and then fresh tomatoes, beetroot and lettuce. Perfect in winter or summer, on a Sunday afternoon.

Serves 4

1 tablespoon olive oil, plus extra,
   for pan-frying
1 small onion, finely diced
1 garlic clove, crushed
1 tablespoon finely chopped
   rosemary
1 tablespoon finely chopped
   flat-leaf (Italian) parsley
500 g (1 lb 2 oz) minced (ground)
   beef or lamb
1 egg
sea salt and freshly ground black
   pepper
hamburger buns, lettuce, tomato,
   beetroot and Tomato Relish
   (page 182), to serve

Heat the oil in a small frying pan over medium–low heat. Add the onion, garlic and half each of the rosemary and parsley. Cook gently, stirring, for 5–6 minutes, or until soft, then remove from the heat. Transfer to a mixing bowl and cool.

Add the remaining rosemary and parsley and the mince and egg to the onion mixture, season with salt and pepper and combine well. Divide the mixture into quarters, shape into balls, then flatten slightly to make four patties. I like my patties quite thick, but it's up to you how thick you make them.

Heat a drizzle of olive oil in a large heavy-based frying pan over medium heat. Cook the patties for 3–4 minutes on each side, or until just cooked through. While the patties are cooking, lightly toast the buns and prepare the fillings.

Serve the patties in the toasted buns, with all the trimmings.

Rosemary Potato Wedges

As well as making a great seasoning for wedges, rosemary salt is also perfect to sprinkle over roast pork, lamb or vegies. You can make the salt ahead of time and store it in an airtight container in the pantry.

Serves 4

1 kg (2 lb 4 oz) all-purpose
   potatoes
2 large rosemary sprigs, leaves
   removed and chopped
grated zest of 1 lemon
80 g (2¾ oz/¼ cup) coarse sea salt
olive oil, for drizzling
2 garlic cloves, crushed
freshly ground black pepper

Preheat the oven to 200°C (400°F).

Cook the unpeeled potatoes in boiling salted water until barely tender. Drain and cut into wedges, leaving the skin on.

Put the rosemary, lemon zest and salt in a mortar and pound with a pestle until a paste forms. If the paste is a little wet, then add a touch more salt.

Put the potato wedges in a roasting tin, drizzle with oil and sprinkle with the garlic. Toss to combine, then sprinkle with some of the rosemary salt and black pepper. Roast, shaking the tin occasionally, for 30 minutes, or until golden all over and crunchy.

Put the remaining rosemary salt on the table for everyone to season their own meals.

Pork with Lemon & Rosemary

While you can prepare and cook this easy dish at the last minute, it's even better if you leave the meat to marinate in the fridge, covered, till the next day. Serve it with Chilli Roast Potatoes (page 186), a green salad or any of the couscous recipes.

Serves 4

1 kg (2 lb 4 oz) pork fillet, sinew removed, cut into 4 even pieces
2 tablespoons olive oil
1 teaspoon finely chopped rosemary
2 tablespoons lemon juice
zest of 1 lemon
sea salt and freshly ground black pepper

Using a meat mallet, gently beat the pork on a chopping board until 1 cm (½ inch) thick. Put the pork in a bowl with all the remaining ingredients and toss to coat well.

Heat a large non-stick frying pan over medium–high heat and cook the pork, in batches, for 2 minutes on each side, or until golden and just cooked through. Rest the pork for 5 minutes, then serve.

If you like them, add a few drained capers to the pan while you're coooking the pork.

Osso Bucco

Perfect for a long informal lunch or cosy winter dinner, let this simmer away while you're entertaining friends on a relaxing Sunday afternoon, filling the house with the most tantalising aroma. And don't forget to eat the delicious marrow - it's the best bit!

Serves 4

75 g (2¾ oz/½ cup) plain
   (all-purpose) flour
sea salt and freshly ground black
   pepper
1.2 kg (2 lb 12 oz) osso bucco
60 ml (2 fl oz/¼ cup) olive oil
100 g (3½ oz) bacon, diced
1 onion, finely chopped
2 garlic cloves, crushed
2 carrots, finely chopped
2 tablespoons thyme leaves
1 tablespoon finely chopped
   rosemary
2 tablespoons finely chopped
   oregano
580 ml (20¼ fl oz/2⅓ cups)
   chicken stock
125 ml (4 fl oz/½ cup) Special
   Tomato Sauce (page 35)
250 ml (9 fl oz/1 cup) red wine
Gremolata (page 61), to serve
   (optional)

Preheat the oven to 150°C (300°F).

Season the flour with salt and pepper. Dust the osso bucco in the flour and shake off any excess. Heat the olive oil in a heavy-based flameproof casserole dish over medium-high heat. Sauté osso bucco until browned on both sides, then remove from the dish.

Add the bacon, onion, garlic, carrot and herbs to the dish, then reduce the heat to medium and stir for 6–8 minutes, or until the carrot is tender. Add the stock, tomato sauce and wine and stir to scrape off any cooked-on pieces from the base of the dish.

Return the meat to the dish and, if necessary, add enough water to just cover the meat. Season to taste, then cover and bake for about 3–4 hours, or until the meat is very tender and falling off the bone.

Serve the osso bucco sprinkled with gremolata, if you like.

Marinated Lamb Kebabs

What I love about lemon and rosemary is that when you leave them to work their magic in a marinade, you can't go wrong. This dish is great for a barbecue with friends or family, or a simple tasty meal at home alone.

Serves 4

800 g (1 lb 12 oz) trimmed lamb
   leg, cut into 2.5 cm (1 inch)
   pieces
juice and grated zest of 1 lemon
1 tablespoon finely chopped
   rosemary
2 garlic cloves, crushed
sea salt and freshly ground black
   pepper
8 woody rosemary stalks with a
   small tip of leaves at the end,
   or bamboo skewers, soaked in
   cold water for 30 minutes

Combine all the ingredients in a bowl, cover and refrigerate for 2–3 hours, or overnight, if time permits.

Thread the lamb pieces onto the skewers, then cook on a lightly oiled, preheated very hot barbecue for about 6–7 minutes, or until cooked to your liking. Rest for 3–4 minutes, then serve.

Don't forget to save your rosemary prunings to make the skewers.

Rosemary Lamb Ragu

I think this truly is my favourite recipe in the book. I try to always have some left over to freeze for another meal, but it really never seems to last that long! It reminds me of rugged-up winter nights and dinner parties with friends. All happy times.

Serves 4

olive oil, for frying
1 leek, pale part only, finely
    chopped
2 carrots, finely chopped
3 garlic cloves, crushed
1 kg (2 lb 4 oz) lamb shoulder, cut
    into large pieces
750 ml (26 fl oz/3 cups) Special
    Tomato Sauce (page 35)
6 rosemary sprigs, leaves only
2 bay leaves
250 ml (9 fl oz/1 cup) vegetable
    stock
250 ml (9 fl oz/1 cup) red wine
sea salt and freshly ground black
    pepper
350 g (12 oz) pasta
grated parmesan cheese, to serve
    (optional)

Preheat the oven to 150°C (300°F).

Heat a little oil in a heavy-based flameproof casserole dish over medium heat. Sauté the leek, carrot and garlic for 7–8 minutes, or until soft, then remove from the dish. Add another drizzle of oil to the dish, increase the heat to high and cook the lamb, in batches, until browned all over, then return all the meat to the dish.

Reduce the heat to low, add the leek mixture, tomato sauce, rosemary, bay leaves, stock and wine and season with salt and pepper.

Simmer for 15 minutes, then cover casserole dish and transfer to the oven. Cook for 3–4 hours, or until the meat is falling apart.

When the ragu is ready, cook pasta in a large saucepan of boiling salted water until *al dente*. Drain and toss through the hot ragu. Serve with grated parmesan, if desired.

Flourless Orange & Rosemary Cake

I love the dense texture of flourless cakes and I love all citrus cakes, so being able to combine the two, with rosemary for extra interest, is an added bonus. I really enjoy using herbs in sweet recipes. It's not a first thought for most home cooks, but it's surprising how well they can work together.

Serves 8

2 oranges
4 eggs
220 g (7¾ oz/1 cup) caster
    (superfine) sugar
200 g (7 oz/2 cups) almond meal
1 teaspoon baking powder
2 tablespoons finely chopped
    rosemary

Preheat the oven to 150°C (300°F). Lightly grease a 15 cm (6 in) round cake tin and line the base with baking paper.

Zest the oranges, then remove the white pith and seeds. Coarsely chop the flesh and put in a food processor with the remaining ingredients. Process until well combined, then pour into the prepared tin. Bake for 40 minutes, or until a skewer inserted into the centre comes out clean.

This cake will brown a little more than usual due to the sugar and juice from the oranges, so if necessary, cover loosely with a piece of foil during baking.

Thyme

Bacon & Egg Bread Cups

Roasted Sweet Potato & Carrot Soup

Rack of Lamb with Herb Crust

Crunchy Herbed Chicken

Lamb Stew

Thyme Dumplings

Thyme Mayonnaise

Thyme Vinaigrette

Lemon & Thyme Cake

Thyme & Lemon Cookies

*T*hyme is another of those hardy herbs that is almost impossible to kill. Pop it in a sunny spot and it will grow all year round, living happily for years, undeterred by neglect or pests and diseases. The only thing that it really doesn't like is constant damp, so make sure that the pot or garden bed is well-drained.

There are literally hundreds of different types of thyme, from neat little bushes to spreading groundcovers. If you have space between the bricks or pavers of your courtyard, one of the creeping thymes can make a lovely scented carpet. Most of the thyme varieties have a similar aroma, but lemon thyme really does have a delicious citrus tang mixed in with the thyme flavour, making it a perfect match for fish or chicken.

The tiny leaves of the thyme plant are usually used whole, although you can also chop them even finer. Unless you are using the very soft new growth, you will also need to strip the leaves off the stalks, as these are woody and not very palatable.

If you have excess thyme, try infusing it in olive oil. Wash and thoroughly dry the sprigs, then add them to a bottle of oil, with a little garlic and chilli, if you like. Leave to infuse for about a week, then strain the oil into a clean, sterilised bottle (page 20).

Flavoured oil for salads and mayonnaise - easy!

Bacon & Egg Bread Cups

Serves 4

2 small vine-ripened tomatoes,
  halved
olive oil, for drizzling
sea salt and freshly ground black
  pepper
8 thyme sprigs
4 slices wholemeal (whole-
  wheat) sandwich bread, crusts
  removed
4 short bacon slices, halved
  lengthways
1 large handful baby English
  spinach leaves
4 eggs

Preheat the oven to 180°C (350°F). Lightly
grease four holes of a 6-hole large size
(Texas/185 ml/6 fl oz/¾ cup) muffin tin.

Put the tomato halves on a baking tray, drizzle
with a little oil, season with salt and pepper and
scatter with half the thyme sprigs. Roast for 20
minutes, or until tender but not falling apart.
Remove from the oven and set aside. Increase
the oven temperature to 200°C (400°F).

Using a rolling pin, roll the bread slices to make
them a little thinner, then press each slice into
the greased muffin tin holes. Bake for about
10 minutes, or just until they begin to brown,
then remove from the oven. Leave oven on.

Put two strips of bacon in each bread cup in
a criss-cross fashion, then put a few spinach
leaves in the base of each and top with a tomato
half. Crack an egg into each mould, being
careful not to break the yolk. Season with salt
and pepper, top with the remaining thyme
sprigs and bake for 15 minutes, or until cooked
to your liking. Serve hot.

Roasted Sweet Potato & Carrot Soup

I stumbled on this dish when I had some leftover roasted vegies. If you're cooking a roast earlier in the week, you could bake all your vegies at the same time. The lovely roasted flavour is what really gives this soup its beautiful depth and velvety taste.

Serves 8

650 g (1 lb 7 oz) sweet potato,
    peeled and coarsely chopped
6 carrots, cut into large chunks
4 garlic cloves, peeled
2 tablespoons olive oil, plus extra,
    for drizzling
2 tablespoons fresh thyme leaves
1 small onion, finely chopped
sea salt and freshly ground black
    pepper

Preheat the oven to 180°C (350°F).

Put the sweet potato, carrot and garlic on a baking tray. Drizzle the vegies with the oil and scatter over 1 tablespoon of the thyme. Roast for 30–40 minutes, or until golden and tender.

Heat the olive oil in a large saucepan over medium heat, add the onion and remaining thyme, and sauté until the onion has softened. Add the roasted vegetables and 2 litres (70 fl oz/8 cups) water. Bring to the boil, then reduce the heat and simmer for 20 minutes, or until the vegetables are very soft.

Using a stick blender, process until smooth, or transfer to a blender and blend in batches. Season to taste with salt and pepper and serve.

A piece of lightly toasted bread on the side is always delicious.

Rack of Lamb with Herb Crust

If you're looking for a special meal, this one will do it. The crust is superb! It really tastes and looks impressive. I've also used it on chicken breasts and roasted them. The crust does not keep for long, so it's best made when you're ready to coat and cook.

Serves 4

2 racks of lamb, 6 cutlets each
1 tablespoon olive oil
sea salt and freshly ground black pepper
60 g (2¼ oz/1 cup) fresh breadcrumbs
2 garlic cloves, crushed
3 tablespoons finely chopped flat-leaf (Italian) parsley
2 teaspoons thyme leaves
½ teaspoon grated lemon zest
40 g (1½ oz) butter, softened

Preheat the oven to 220°C (425°F).

Score the fat on the lamb racks in a diamond pattern, then rub with the oil and season with salt and pepper.

Heat a large frying pan over medium–high heat. Cook the lamb racks, fat side down, for 3–4 minutes, or until a lot of the fat has rendered, then remove the racks from the pan and leave to cool a little.

Meanwhile, combine the breadcrumbs, garlic, parsley, thyme and lemon zest in a bowl and season to taste. Add the butter and mix well.

Firmly press the breadcrumb mixture over the fat on the racks, leaving the bones and base clean. Put the racks on a baking tray and bake for about 12 minutes for medium-rare, or to your liking. Rest for 5–6 minutes before slicing.

Crunchy Herbed Chicken

My different spin on a chicken schnitzel. Although it's best served as soon as it is cooked, it's also delicious cold, dolloped with mayonnaise.

Serves 4

120 g (4¼ oz/2 cups) fresh
   breadcrumbs
6 thyme sprigs, leaves removed
grated zest of 1 lemon
1 teaspoon finely chopped
   fresh long red chilli, seeded
   (optional)
4 skinless chicken breast fillets
75 g (2¾ oz/½ cup) plain
   (all-purpose) flour
1 egg, lightly whisked
sea salt and freshly ground black
   pepper
olive oil, for pan-frying
lemon cheeks, to serve

Preheat the oven to 180°C (350°F).

In a shallow bowl, combine the breadcrumbs, thyme leaves, lemon zest and chilli, if using.

Using a meat mallet, gently pound the chicken breasts until they are lightly flattened and an even thickness all over. Put the flour and egg in separate shallow bowls and season the flour with salt and pepper.

Dust the chicken breasts in the seasoned flour, shaking off any excess, then dip in the beaten egg and coat with the breadcrumbs.

Heat 1 cm (½ inch) oil in an ovenproof frying pan over medium heat. Sauté the chicken breasts until golden all over, then transfer the pan to the oven and bake for 15 minutes, or until just cooked through. Leave to rest for 5 minutes, before serving with lemon cheeks.

Lamb Stew

Serves 4

2 tablespoons olive oil

700 g (1 lb 9 oz) trimmed lamb leg
or shoulder, cut into 2 cm
(¾ inch) pieces

1 onion, finely chopped

2 garlic cloves, crushed

250 ml (9 fl oz/1 cup) Special
Tomato Sauce (page 35)

1 bay leaf

3 thyme sprigs

1 tablespoon finely chopped
flat-leaf (Italian) parsley

2 rosemary sprigs, leaves
removed and finely chopped

500 ml (17 fl oz/2 cups) vegetable
stock

400 g (14 oz) all-purpose
potatoes, peeled and cut into
chunks

1 carrot, coarsely chopped

sea salt and freshly ground black
pepper

140 g (5 oz/1 cup) frozen peas

GARLIC CRUMBS

80 ml (2½ fl oz/⅓ cup) olive oil

2 garlic cloves, crushed

20 g (¾ oz/⅓ cup) fresh
breadcrumbs

Heat the olive oil in a heavy-based saucepan
over high heat. Sauté the lamb, in two batches,
until golden all over. Remove from the pan,
reduce the heat to low and add the onion and
garlic. Sauté for 5–6 minutes, or until the onion
is soft, then return the lamb to the pan.

Add the tomato sauce, herbs, stock, potato,
carrot and a splash of water, then season with
salt and pepper. Cover the pan and simmer for
25 minutes, or until the meat is nearly tender.
Stir in the peas and simmer, uncovered, for a
further 10 minutes, or until the lamb is tender.

Meanwhile, for the garlic crumbs, heat the olive
oil and garlic in a small frying pan over low
heat. Add the breadcrumbs and stir until golden
and crisp. Drain on paper towel.

Serve stew sprinkled with the garlic crumbs.

This stew is
delicious with
Thyme Dumplings
(page 154).

Thyme Dumplings

Dumplings are a great accompaniment to any slow-cooked meal, be it casserole or soup – I love serving them with my Lamb Stew (page 153). You can cook them, then cool and freeze them for up to three months.

Makes 24 (mini muffin size)

300 g (10½ oz/2 cups) plain (all-purpose) flour, plus extra, for dusting

1 tablespoon baking powder

1 tablespoon sugar

1 teaspoon salt

2 tablespoons thyme leaves, finely chopped

160 g (5¾ oz) butter, softened, plus extra, for greasing

185 ml (6½ fl oz/¾ cup) buttermilk

1 egg, lightly whisked

Preheat the oven to 200°C (400°F). Lightly grease a 24-hole mini muffin tin.

Combine all the dry ingredients and thyme in a large bowl. Add the softened butter, then the buttermilk and egg and stir until just combined.

Turn out onto a lightly floured work surface and knead just until the dough comes together. Divide the dough into 24 pieces and roll into balls. Put the dough balls into the greased muffin holes and bake for 12 minutes, or until just cooked through.

Warm up defrosted dumplings for a few minutes in the oven before serving.

Thyme Mayonnaise

Mayonnaise is always a great condiment to keep in the fridge. Use it for sandwiches, as a dressing for green salads or a dip for crispy potato wedges. A favourite trick of mine is to spread a little over cold Crunchy Herbed Chicken (page 151) and wrap the whole thing in lettuce. Yum!

*Makes 235 g
(8½ oz / 1 cup)*

1 egg, at room temperature
¾ teaspoon salt
1 tablespoon white vinegar
½ teaspoon dijon mustard
pinch of cayenne pepper
3 tablespoons thyme leaves
1 garlic clove, finely chopped
250 ml (9 fl oz/1 cup) vegetable oil

Put all the ingredients, except the oil, in the bowl of a blender or food processor and process until smooth.

With the motor running, gradually add the oil, drop by drop at first and then in a slow steady stream until the mixture becomes thick, glossy and emulsified.

Check the seasoning and adjust with a little extra salt or vinegar, if needed.

Keep mayonnaise in an airtight container in the fridge, for up to 1 week.

Thyme Vinaigrette

It's always great to have the time to make your dressing fresh, whenever you need it, but I always make extra so I can quickly dress a salad for a lazy meal later in the week, when I really don't have the time or energy. This dressing will keep refrigerated in an airtight jar for up to one week.

*Makes 185 ml
(6 fl oz / ¾ cup)*

125 ml (4 fl oz/½ cup) olive oil
60 ml (2 fl oz/¼ cup) lemon juice
½ teaspoon wholegrain mustard
1 teaspoon thyme leaves
sea salt and freshly ground black
   pepper

Combine all the ingredients in a jar, seal and shake well to combine.

This is the perfect dressing for a simple green salad to accompany grilled meat or chicken.

Lemon & Thyme Cake

*If you're looking for something a little different, why not try this cake?
I love the tanginess of the lemon here, but it's not quite as lemony as the
cakes in the Lemon chapter, to allow for the subtle taste of the thyme.
Great served warm with a cuppa and friends!*

Serves 6

200 g (7 oz) unsalted butter,
    slightly softened
200 g (7 oz) sugar
100 g (3½ oz/⅔ cup) plain
    (all-purpose) flour
½ teaspoon baking powder
100 g (3½ oz/1 cup) almond meal
4 eggs, at room temperature
grated zest of 1 lemon
1 teaspoon thyme leaves, finely
    chopped
icing (confectioners') sugar, for
    dusting
lemon syrup (*see* Lemon Polenta
    Cake, page 208), to serve
    (optional)
thick (double) cream, to serve

Preheat the oven to 160°C (315°F). Lightly grease an 18 cm (7 inch) round cake tin and line the base and side with baking paper.

Using an electric mixer, cream the butter and sugar together until pale and creamy. Sift the flour and baking powder together, then add to the butter mixture with the almond meal.

Add the eggs, one at a time, beating well after each addition, then add the lemon zest and thyme and combine well. Pour into the prepared tin and bake for 40 minutes, or until a skewer inserted into the centre comes out clean. Stand in the tin for 5 minutes, then turn out.

Dust the top with icing sugar and serve warm or at room temperature, with lemon syrup, if using, and thick cream.

Thyme & Lemon Cookies

Lemon and thyme is a delicious and unusual flavour combination in these light and lovely cookies. They are best eaten straight away, of course, but will keep in an airtight container for up to 1 week.

Makes 36

100 g (3½ oz) unsalted butter,
   slightly softened
165 g (5¾ oz/¾ cup) sugar
1 egg, at room temperature,
   lightly whisked
½ teaspoon natural vanilla
   extract
1 tablespoon milk
1 teaspoon grated lemon zest
1 tablespoon thyme leaves
185 g (6½ oz/1¼ cups) plain
   (all-purpose) flour
¼ teaspoon baking powder
pinch of salt

Using an electric mixer, beat the butter and sugar together until pale and creamy. Add the egg, vanilla and milk and combine well, then stir through the lemon zest and thyme.

Sift the flour, baking powder and salt into a bowl, then add to the butter mixture and stir until well combined. Roll out the dough between two sheets of baking paper until it is about 5 mm (¼ inch) thick. If you need to roll the dough in two lots, stack the layers on baking trays. Refrigerate for 30 minutes.

Preheat the oven to 180°C (350°F). Line two baking trays with baking paper.

Using a 5 cm (2 inch) round cutter, cut out rounds of chilled dough and put on the prepared trays. Bake for 10 minutes, or until lightly browned. Re-roll the scraps and repeat. Cool on wire racks, then store in an airtight container for up to 1 week.

Chilli

Marinated Olives

Pad Thai Rice

Chilli Vegie Tagine

Red Curry Paste

Beef Pilaf

Sweet Chilli Sauce

Dad's Chilli Sauce

Tomato Relish

Barbecued Whole Snapper

Chilli Roast Potatoes

Chilli Chocolate Molten Puddings

I *find people either love chilli or hate it. I grew up with parents who both love spicy food, so I've tried all degrees of spicy. I like a little chilli, but not so much that I can't enjoy the meal. There are so many varieties of chilli - some extremely hot and others quite mild - that you can grow whichever ones suit you best. When using hot chilli, you can always decrease the heat a little by discarding the seeds.*

What I love about chilli is that it goes surprisingly well with sweet flavours as well as savoury. I love the excitement in my mouth that you get with chilli and chocolate. I've included a decadent pudding in this chapter, but I first had chilli with chocolate in a hot chocolate drink. Chilli also goes really well with most other herbs: it's commonly used with parsley, basil, rosemary and coriander (cilantro).

The other great thing about chilli is that the bushes are so pretty, with the fruit coming in an array of colours, from fire-engine red to yellow, orange, green and purple. They look gorgeous – even if you don't want to eat them!

To store your chillies, keep them in the fridge in a ziplock bag, where they will keep for up to a month. But they also freeze really well – I keep a few there for emergencies and they defrost within minutes.

Marinated Olives

I always serve olives when friends are over, especially in winter, when warm olives are just perfect. They really get your taste buds going and make something special of a quick appetiser. They can be prepared in advance, and heated just before your guests arrive.

Serves 6 as an appetiser

350 g (12 oz/2 cups) mixed
    unpitted olives
½ teaspoon seeded and finely
    chopped fresh long red chilli
1 tablespoon finely chopped fresh
    oregano
125 ml (4 fl oz/½ cup) balsamic
    vinegar
60 ml (2 fl oz/¼ cup) olive oil
1 garlic clove, crushed

Put all the ingredients in a large frying pan and stir over low heat until heated through.

Transfer to a serving bowl and allow to stand for 10 minutes to cool slightly before serving.

I usually have olives marinating in the fridge at all times - I love them!

Pad Thai Rice

After spending some time in Thailand, I was inspired to learn about the food and was lucky enough to do a Thai cooking class. The food is always so fresh and it makes you feel like you're on holidays just eating it! Since I'm not a huge fan of noodles, I prefer this rice version.

Serves 4

2 tablespoons vegetable oil
I egg, lightly whisked
½ teaspoon sesame oil
I tablespoon finely grated fresh
   ginger
I garlic clove, crushed
2 fresh long red chillies, seeded
   and finely chopped
740 g (I lb IO oz/4 cups) cooked
   jasmine rice
I tablespoon soy sauce
I tablespoon fish sauce
I tablespoon lime juice
finely chopped spring onion
   (scallions), to serve
chopped toasted peanuts, to serve

Heat I teaspoon of the oil in a large wok over medium–high heat. Add the egg and swirl over the wok to cover as much surface area as possible. Cook for 30 seconds, then remove the omelette from the wok and chop it finely.

Heat the remaining oil in the wok over medium–high heat, add the sesame oil, ginger, garlic and chilli and stir-fry for about 30 seconds, or until fragrant. Add the cooked rice, soy sauce, fish sauce and lime juice and stir until heated through. Stir through the omelette and serve the rice with spring onions and peanuts scattered over the top.

For a more substantial meal, stir-fry chicken or prawns (shrimp) before adding the rice.

Chilli Vegie Tagine

Serves 4

1 tablespoon olive oil
1 onion, finely chopped
2 garlic cloves, crushed
1 teaspoon ground cumin
1 teaspoon sumac
1 teaspoon ground coriander
1 fresh long red chilli, finely
    chopped
1 x 400 g (14 oz) tin diced
    tomatoes
½ teaspoon sugar
1 x 400 g (14 oz) tin lentils,
    drained and rinsed
500 g (1 lb 2 oz) pumpkin (winter
    squash), peeled and cut into
    4 cm (1½ inch) pieces
500 g (1 lb 2 oz) sweet potato,
    peeled and cut into 4 cm
    (1½ inch) pieces
500 g (1 lb 2 oz) potato, cut into
    4 cm (1½ inch) pieces
250 ml (9 fl oz/1 cup) vegetable
    stock
1 handful flat-leaf (Italian)
    parsley leaves
1 handful coriander (cilantro)
    leaves
sea salt and freshly ground black
    pepper
prepared couscous, to serve

Heat the olive oil in a heavy-based saucepan over medium heat. Add the onion and garlic and cook for 5–6 minutes, or until soft.

Add the ground spices and chilli and cook for 2–3 minutes, or until fragrant. Add the tomatoes, sugar, lentils, vegetables, stock and half the herbs.

Reduce the heat to low, cover and cook for 1 hour, or until the vegetables are tender, but not mushy. Season with salt and pepper, then gently stir in the remaining herbs, reserving a little to scatter over the top. Serve with couscous.

Although this is a meal in itself, it also makes a great side dish for roast beef or chicken.

Red Curry Paste

I always have a variety of pastes in the fridge ready to go, as they keep really well - although mine never last longer than a month! It's a great way to use up extra chillies. To make a lovely Thai-style curry, simply fry off a tablespoon or two of this curry paste in a little vegetable oil, add coconut milk and your favourite vegies or meat and simmer until tender.

Makes about 250 g (9 oz/1 cup)

1 teaspoon cumin seeds

2 teaspoons coriander seeds

½ teaspoon black peppercorns

½ teaspoon salt

12 fresh long red chillies, seeded and finely chopped

1 teaspoon finely grated fresh galangal

1 lemongrass stalk, white part only, finely chopped

4 kaffir lime leaves, finely chopped

2 shallots, finely chopped

4 garlic cloves, crushed

1 teaspoon shrimp paste

6 red bird's eye chillies (optional)

Put the cumin and coriander seeds and the peppercorns in a small dry frying pan and shake over low heat for 3–4 minutes, or until fragrant. Remove from the heat and cool, then grind finely using a mortar and pestle.

Put the ground spices in a blender with all the remaining ingredients and process until a paste forms. Transfer to a jar or other airtight container. This paste will keep in the fridge for up to 1 week, or frozen, for up to 1 month.

You can also use this paste to brush over meat or chicken skewers before cooking on the barbecue.

Beef Pilaf

As this recipe uses minced beef, it is relatively inexpensive to make. It's also quick to cook, which makes it a great weeknight meal.

Serves 4

1½ tablespoons olive oil
500 g (1 lb 2 oz) minced (ground) beef
½ teaspoon ground cumin
½ teaspoon mild paprika
½ teaspoon ground turmeric
1 teaspoon seeded and finely chopped fresh long red chilli
1 small onion, finely chopped
300 g (10½ oz/1½ cups) basmati rice
750 ml (26 fl oz/3 cups) vegetable stock
80 g (2¾ oz/½ cup) fresh or frozen peas
2 large tomatoes, diced
50 g (1¾ oz/¼ cup) sultanas (golden raisins)
1 handful flat-leaf (Italian) parsley leaves, chopped, plus extra, to serve
sea salt and freshly ground black pepper

Heat 2 teaspoons of the oil in a heavy-based saucepan over high heat. Add the beef and cook, breaking up any lumps with the back of a spoon, until browned. Transfer the beef to a bowl and set aside.

Heat the remaining oil in the same pan over medium heat. Add the spices and chilli and cook for 30 seconds, or until fragrant, then add the onion and stir for 5–6 minutes, or until soft.

Add the rice and stir to coat, then pour in the stock and bring to the boil. Reduce the heat to as low as possible, cover with a tight-fitting lid and cook for 15 minutes. Remove from the heat and allow to stand for another 15 minutes, without removing the lid.

Stir through the beef and all the remaining ingredients with a fork, season to taste and serve with extra parsley scattered over the top.

Sweet Chilli Sauce

I love homemade sweet chilli sauce. I always have extra, so I never need to buy it. As long as you make sure your jars are well sterilised, it will keep, unopened, for at least two years. If you don't like your sauce too hot, then remove the seeds from half the chillies before you start this recipe.

*Makes about 500 ml
(17 fl oz/ 2 cups)*

125 g (4½ oz) fresh long red
   chillies
4 garlic cloves
2 teaspoons finely grated fresh
   ginger
60 ml (2 fl oz/¼ cup) white
   vinegar
330 g (11¾ oz/1½ cups) sugar
2 teaspoons salt

Process the chillies, garlic and ginger in a food processor until finely chopped. Slowly add the vinegar and process until a paste forms.

Transfer the mixture to a saucepan, then add the sugar, salt and 185 ml (6 fl oz/¾ cup) water. Bring to the boil over medium heat, then reduce the heat to low and simmer, stirring occasionally, for 45 minutes, or until the sauce is reduced and thickened. Pour into hot sterilised jars (page 20) and seal.

I love to include my Sweet Chilli Sauce in a Christmas gift hamper, along with other sauces and jams I've made.

Dad's Chilli Sauce

I remember my dad cooking this recipe when I was a child, and the excitement on his face. It seemed to take all day and was like a science to him, as he checked and tasted. This sauce is extra extra hot. If you prefer it a little milder, then use long red chillies instead of bird's eyes.

*Makes about 500 g
(1 lb 2 oz/ 2 cups)*

500 g (1 lb 2 oz) fresh red bird's
    eye chillies
100 ml (3½ fl oz) vegetable oil
6 garlic cloves, crushed
1 teaspoon finely grated fresh
    ginger
220 ml (7¾ fl oz) tomato passata
    (puréed tomatoes)
2 tablespoons sugar, or to taste

A small dollop will spice up any meal – it's especially good with bangers and mash!

Process the chillies in a food processor until finely chopped.

Place a wok over medium heat and add the oil and garlic. Stir for 30 seconds, or just until starting to brown. Add the ginger and cook for 1 minute, then add the chopped chilli and stir for a further 5 minutes. Add the tomato passata and, as soon as the mixture starts to bubble, add 125 ml (4 fl oz/½ cup) water.

Cook, stirring occasionally, for about 2 hours, or until the chilli breaks down into a paste. My dad says to wait until the oil comes to the surface. Depending on your chillies and their age, you may need to add the sugar, but it is really a question of personal taste.

Spoon the hot sauce into hot sterilised jars (page 20) and seal. The sauce will keep unopened in a cool, dark place for up to 2 years.

Tomato Relish

My favourite way to eat this relish is on a BLT with avocado. I haven't met a single person who doesn't love it - I'm always getting asked for a jar. It's like gold in my fridge!

Makes about 1 kg
(2 lb 4 oz/ 4 cups)

2 kg (4 lb 8 oz) ripe tomatoes
30 g (1 oz) fresh ginger, finely chopped
30 g (1 oz) garlic cloves, crushed
60 g (2¼ oz) fresh long red chillies, finely chopped
360 g (12¾ oz/1⅔ cups) sugar
55 g (2 oz/¼ cup) salt
260 ml (9½ fl oz) white vinegar

Using a small sharp knife, score the base of each tomato, then remove the core. Drop the tomatoes into a large saucepan of boiling water for 30 seconds, then remove with a slotted spoon and place in a large bowl of iced water. Drain, then peel and cut into large chunks.

Put the tomatoes and all the remaining ingredients in a heavy-based saucepan. Bring to the boil, then reduce the heat and simmer, stirring occasionally, for 1 hour, or until thick.

Spoon the hot relish into hot sterilised jars (page 20) and seal. Store in a cool, dark place for at least 2 weeks before opening. Once it has been opened, the relish will keep, refrigerated, for up to 1 month.

Sealed relish can be stored for up to 12 months.

Barbecued Whole Snapper

I cook this dish when I've got a group of people coming over, as it's easy to prepare and wrap the fish beforehand and still have time to enjoy everyone's company. It works just as well for dinner for one, of course.

Serves 4

4 plate-sized snapper, about
    2 kg (4 lb 8 oz) in total, cleaned
    and scaled
90 g (3¼ oz/1 bunch) coriander
    (cilantro), including roots,
    stalks and leaves, well rinsed
    and finely chopped
2 fresh long red chillies, seeded
    and finely chopped
2 limes, thinly sliced
sea salt and freshly ground black
    pepper

Cut three slits into each side of each fish but not all the way through. Place a little of each of the three remaining ingredients into each slit and place the rest into the fish cavities. Season with salt and pepper, both inside and out.

Wrap the fish individually in baking paper, then foil (or a large piece of banana leaf, if you can get it). Cook on a preheated hot barbecue, with the lid closed, for 5 minutes on each side, or just until cooked through.

Decorate your cooked fish with lots of fresh herb sprigs.

Chilli Roast Potatoes

If you like to think of different ways to serve potatoes, then try this recipe with a little kick of spice. Serve as a side to any cooked meats or for something special to go with your Sunday roast.

Serves 4

1 kg (2 lb 4 oz) all-purpose potatoes, peeled and cut into wedges
4 garlic cloves, finely chopped
2 fresh long red chillies, seeded and finely chopped
60 ml (2 fl oz/¼ cup) olive oil
sea salt and freshly ground black pepper

Preheat the oven to 200°C (400°F).

Put all the ingredients in a roasting tin and toss to coat well with the oil. Roast, turning them occasionally, for 40–45 minutes, or until golden and crisp all over.

Your potatoes will cook up even crisper if you parboil them until barely tender, then drain, before roasting.

Chilli Chocolate Molten Puddings

When you're looking for something special to share with friends after dinner, this combination of chilli and chocolate is really lovely. There's not a lot of preparation - it's all in the timing of the cooking. The puddings should have a nice crust on top, but still be soft and gooey in the middle.

Serves 4

170 g (6 oz) good-quality, dark chocolate (70% cocoa solids)
150 g (5½ oz) unsalted butter, plus extra, for greasing
3 eggs, at room temperature
160 g (5¾ oz) caster (superfine) sugar
1 fresh long red chilli, seeded and finely chopped
75 g (2¾ oz/½ cup) plain (all-purpose) flour
1 vanilla bean, halved lengthways and seeds scraped
icing (confectioners') sugar and unsweetened cocoa powder, for dusting
whipped cream, to serve

Preheat the oven to 190°C (375°F). Lightly grease four 250 ml (9 fl oz/1 cup) ramekins.

Melt the chocolate and butter in a heatproof bowl over a saucepan of barely simmering water, making sure base of bowl does not touch the water, then remove from the heat and allow to cool slightly.

Using an electric mixer, whisk the eggs and sugar until thick and pale. Add the chocolate mixture, chilli, flour and vanilla seeds and combine well. Pour into the prepared ramekins and bake for 8 minutes. At the start of the seventh minute, check to see if the crust is baked enough: not too brittle, but still a little wobbly, as the centre should still be liquid. If it is under-baked, continue for another minute.

Lightly dust with combined icing sugar and cocoa and serve warm with whipped cream.

Lemon

Quick Lemon & Thyme Chicken

Roast Vegies with Lemon

Lemon Fish

Crispy Chicken with Lemon Sauce

Lemon Vinaigrette

Tangy Carrot Salad

Barbecued Prawn Skewers

Lemon Polenta Cake

Lemon Curd Tarts

Lemon Butter Biscuits

I love the versatility of lemons and I think every garden or courtyard should always have a lemon tree, if possible. They can be used for their juice, fruit or skin, they go well with chilli, coriander, thyme, parsley and rosemary and the tangy flavour of lemon works brilliantly in both savoury and sweet recipes.

The scent of the blossom on a lemon tree is quite beautiful in spring, and then you get a wonderfully generous crop of fruit, that lasts for ages on the tree, or stores well when picked. Once your lemons have ripened, they will keep on the shelf for about a month. I generally don't keep them in the fridge, but you could easily store them there to extend their life.

And of course, you can freeze both the juice and the zest in small amounts for adding to recipes as needed. You can also freeze lemon slices for adding to drinks in summer.

There is a type of lemon tree to suit most climates, from those that thrive in mild conditions, magically producing fruit all year round – that's the sort I have – to those that will withstand colder weather, but have a more defined period of production. There are even dwarf varieties that are specially adapted for pots – so if you've got a sunny spot in your courtyard, what are you waiting for?

Lemons are just so useful and I include them whenever I can.

Quick Lemon & Thyme Chicken

When you haven't got much time and are looking for a tasty meal, look no further. I've sometimes marinated this for only 20 minutes and it's still full of flavour. You can cook it on the barbecue or a chargrill pan, or even just pan-fry it and serve with any salad that takes your fancy.

Serves 4

600 g (1 lb 5 oz) chicken
    tenderloins
4 thyme sprigs
juice of 1 lemon
sea salt and freshly ground black
    pepper

Put the chicken, thyme and lemon juice in a bowl and combine well. Cover and refrigerate for 2–3 hours, if time permits.

Season the chicken with salt and pepper, then cook on a lightly oiled preheated hot barbecue for 2 minutes on each side, or until lightly golden and just cooked through.

Tenderloins are a lovely cut of chicken, but do take care not to overcook them or they will be tough.

Roast Vegies with Lemon

With a lovely lemony zing that really gets your taste buds fired up, this is a great accompaniment to any roasted meats. You can combine the herbs and spices with the olive oil days in advance and store in an airtight container, ready for drizzling over your vegie combination.

Serves 4 as a side

600 g (1 lb 5 oz) all-purpose potatoes, peeled and cut into large chunks

500 g (1 lb 2 oz) pumpkin (winter squash), peeled and cut into large chunks

2 large carrots, peeled and quartered

250 g (9 oz) sweet potato, peeled and cut into large chunks

1 onion, peeled and quartered

6 garlic cloves

4 bay leaves

2 lemons, quartered

½ teaspoon sumac

½ teaspoon chilli flakes

1 teaspoon thyme leaves

80 ml (2½ fl oz/⅓ cup) olive oil

sea salt and freshly ground black pepper

Preheat the oven to 200°C (400°F).

Put all the ingredients in a large roasting tin, season with salt and pepper and toss to combine well.

Roast for 45–50 minutes, turning occasionally, until golden and tender.

If you like them, add other root vegies to the mix, such as parsnip and swede (rutabaga).

Lemon Fish

This is not so much a recipe as a delicious, healthy, low-fat way to serve a simple piece of fish. Use only the very freshest fish fillet - it should smell of the sea - and take care not to overcook it. The result, when you open the parcel, will be moist and delicately lemon-infused.

Serves 1

175 g (6 oz) firm white fish fillet, skin removed
sea salt and freshly ground black pepper
2 lemon slices
1 teaspoon olive oil (optional)
coriander (cilantro) or flat-leaf (Italian) parsley leaves, to garnish

Preheat the oven to 180°C (350°F).

Cut a piece of baking paper big enough to wrap around your piece of fish.

Put the fish in the centre of the paper, season with salt and pepper and top with the lemon slices. Drizzle with oil, if using. Wrap up the fish to make a parcel, then place on a baking tray and bake for 7 minutes, or until just cooked.

Garnish with fresh herbs to serve.

For a change, try adding chilli, spring onions (scallions) or fresh herbs before wrapping.

Crispy Chicken with Lemon Sauce

I like to use extra lemon in everything and this is extra tangy. I love it that way. This dish doesn't keep well, but that's fine, as you won't have any left over anyway! If you prefer less bite, grind the peppercorns more finely.

Serves 2

2 tablespoons cornflour
   (cornstarch)
I teaspoon salt
I tablespoon sichuan
   peppercorns, coarsely ground
I egg, lightly whisked
vegetable oil, for deep-frying
300 g (10½ oz) skinless chicken
   breast fillets, cut into 2 cm
   (¾ in) pieces
steamed rice, to serve

LEMON SAUCE
grated zest and juice of 2 lemons
45 g (1½ oz/⅓ cup) grated palm
   sugar (jaggery)

For the lemon sauce, put the juice, zest and sugar in a small saucepan and stir over low heat until the sugar dissolves. Bring to the boil, then remove from the heat and set aside until ready to reheat just before serving.

Combine the cornflour, salt and sichuan pepper on a plate or in a shallow bowl. Put the whisked egg in a shallow bowl.

Heat the oil in a deep-fryer or large saucepan to 180°C (350°F), or until a cube of bread dropped into the oil turns golden brown in 15 seconds.

Working in small batches, dip the chicken in the egg, drain the excess, then dust in the cornflour mixture. Cook for 2–3 minutes, or until golden and crisp, then drain on paper towel.

Serve the chicken with the lemon sauce and steamed rice.

Lemon Vinaigrette

I always have a salad dressing in the fridge, ready to go. Whether you're quickly pan-frying chicken breasts or throwing some fish on the barbecue, there will always be a salad to go on the side and this classic vinaigrette is my favourite go-to dressing. Add chopped herbs for a change, if you like.

Makes 125 ml
(4 fl oz/½ cup)

2 tablespoons balsamic vinegar
2 tablespoons honey
1 tablespoon lemon juice
125 ml (4 fl oz/½ cup) olive oil
sea salt and freshly ground black
    pepper

Put all the ingredients in a jar, seal and shake until emulsified.

This vinaigrette will keep refrigerated in an airtight container for up to 1 week.

Tangy Carrot Salad

Surprise your friends with this salad at your next party. I find I'm often left with lots of carrots in the fridge and this simple, fresh, slightly spicy salad is a great way to use them up.

Serves 4

2 large carrots, peeled
2 tablespoons finely chopped
    flat-leaf (Italian) parsley

DRESSING
I garlic clove, crushed
¼ teaspoon ground cumin or mild
    paprika
80 ml (2½ fl oz/⅓ cup) olive oil
I teaspoon white wine vinegar
I teaspoon honey
juice of ½ lemon
sea salt and freshly ground black
    pepper

For the dressing, put all the ingredients in a jar, seal and shake until emulsified.

Using a vegetable peeler or mandolin, slice the carrots lengthways into thin ribbons. Put in a bowl, pour over the dressing and toss gently. Scatter over the parsley to serve.

This salad is best eaten as soon as you've added the dressing.

Barbecued Prawn Skewers

Everyone loves a prawn, and these are equally delightful on the barbecue or cooked inside on a chargrill pan. This is an easy meal that can be prepared in advance of your guests arriving, with just the quick cooking left to do when everyone is ready to eat.

Serves 4-6

½ lemon
2 garlic cloves, crushed
I fresh long red chilli, seeded and finely chopped
I handful mint leaves, finely chopped
I tablespoon olive oil
24 raw king prawns (shrimp), peeled and deveined, leaving the tails intact
sea salt and freshly ground black pepper
8–12 bamboo skewers, soaked in cold water for 30 minutes
lemon wedges, to serve (optional)

Grate the zest from the half lemon, then juice it.

In a bowl, combine the garlic, chilli, mint, lemon zest and juice and olive oil. Add the prawns and toss to coat. Cover with plastic wrap and transfer to the fridge for 10 minutes, to allow the flavours to develop.

Thread 2–3 prawns onto each skewer and season with salt and pepper. Cook on a hot barbecue plate or chargrill pan for 2–3 minutes on each side, or until just cooked through. Take care not to overcook them.

Serve with lemon wedges, if you like.

Lemon Polenta Cake

The syrup for this cake is very lemony, so if you prefer it a little less tart, just reduce the amount of lemon juice or add a little more sugar to taste. Pour the syrup over the cake just before serving – it is especially lovely when still slightly warm. The cake will keep for up to one week.

Serves 4–6

2 lemons
200 g (7 oz) unsalted butter, at
    room temperature
200 g (7 oz) caster (superfine)
    sugar
100 g (3½ oz/1 cup) almond meal
100 g (3½ oz) fine polenta
    (cornmeal)
3 eggs, at room temperature,
    lightly whisked
2 teaspoons baking powder
thick (double) cream, to serve

LEMON SYRUP
juice of 2 lemons
165 g (5¾ oz/¾ cup) caster
    (superfine) sugar

Preheat the oven to 160°C (315°F). Grease and line the base and side of a 20 cm (8 inch) round cake tin with baking paper.

Zest both the lemons, then juice one of them.

Using an electric mixer, cream the butter and sugar until pale and creamy. Add the almond meal and polenta, then stir in eggs and baking powder. Add lemon zest and juice and stir until just combined, then spoon into the prepared tin.

Bake for 1 hour, or until a skewer inserted into the centre comes out clean. If you find the top is browning too quickly, cover the tin loosely with foil during baking.

Meanwhile, for the lemon syrup, put the juice and sugar in a small saucepan and stir over low heat until sugar dissolves. Simmer, stirring, for 5 minutes, then remove from the heat and cool.

Serve the cake, warm or cold, with cream and lemon syrup poured over just before serving.

Lemon Curd Tarts

Spooned into store-bought pastry cases, homemade lemon curd makes a great last-minute dessert or a lovely quick treat for friends who have popped over for tea. A little jar of it also makes a nice gourmet gift.

Makes 225 g (8 oz/1 cup) of lemon curd

purchased pastry cases

LEMON CURD
3 lemons
220 g (7¾ oz/1 cup) caster (superfine) sugar
110 g (3¾ oz) unsalted butter, chopped
3 eggs, lightly whisked

For the lemon curd, zest one of the lemons, then juice all of them. Put the zest, sugar and butter in a small saucepan and stir over low heat until the sugar dissolves.

Whisk together the lemon juice and egg, then add to the butter mixture and stir until the mixture thickens enough to coat the back of a wooden spoon. Do not boil the mixture or the egg will scramble.

Strain the curd through a fine sieve, then pour into sterilised jars (page 20) and seal.

Spoon a small amount of lemon curd into each pastry case and serve immediately.

Lemon curd will keep, refrigerated, for up to 2 weeks.

Lemon Butter Biscuits

I love lemon and I love biscuits. So, together, these are heaven! I remember my grandmother always having something homemade in the pantry. Baking was a weekly ritual, because she said you always had to have something ready in case anyone popped in for a cuppa and a chat.

Makes 36 unfilled biscuits

250 g (9 oz) unsalted butter,
   softened
125 g (4½ oz/1 cup) icing
   (confectioners') sugar, sifted
300 g (10½ oz/2 cups) plain
   (all-purpose) flour
1 quantity chilled Lemon Curd
   (page 211)

*Unfilled biscuits
will keep in an
airtight container
for up to 3 days.*

Preheat the oven to 180°C (350°F). Line two baking trays with baking paper.

Using an electric mixer, cream the butter and icing sugar until pale and creamy. Add the flour and stir until just combined. Transfer to a lightly floured work surface and knead the dough very briefly, just until it comes together. Shape into a disc, cover with plastic wrap, then refrigerate for 30 minutes.

Roll out the dough on a lightly floured work surface until 5 mm (¼ inch) thick. Using a 5 cm (2 inch) round cutter, cut out biscuits and place on prepared trays. Bake for 10 minutes, or until very lightly coloured. Gently re-roll the scraps and repeat the cutting and baking. Cool biscuits on the trays for 5 minutes, then transfer to a wire rack to cool completely.

Spoon a little lemon curd onto half the biscuits, then sandwich with remaining biscuits.

Strawberry

Strawberry Fizz

Strawberry, Mint & Ginger Syrup

Strawberry Nests

Apple & Strawberry Crumble

Strawberry Tarts

Strawberry Jam

*S*trawberries might seem an unlikely choice for a courtyard garden, but I do love to grow them. I never seem to be able to collect a large number for cooking, as I always pick and eat them straight off the plant, as soon as they ripen. There's nothing better than a sun-drenched fresh strawberry, straight from your garden.

There's also a wonderful sense of triumph in beating the birds, slugs and snails to that one perfectly ripe piece of fruit!

But even if you only have a small space, there's no reason why you can't grow enough strawberries to use. To grow multiple plants in the one pot, you can buy special strawberry pots with little 'pockets', that allow extra plants – and their fruit – to hang off the side. These pots look very pretty in full bloom, and have the added advantage of keeping the fruit off the ground and away from pests and soil-borne diseases. Just make sure the pot is well fed and watered, to sustain the multiple inhabitants.

You can also hang a pot of strawberries, which not only looks decorative and is ideal for small spaces, but it will also keep the plants out of reach of slugs and snails. I have never had to spray or treat my hanging strawberries and they have never been eaten – except by me.

Even if you only grow enough for a single bowl of homegrown strawberries and cream, it will be worth it!

Strawberry Fizz

A pretty and refreshing drink on a hot summer's day, this is superb for a picnic. Try mixing all the liquids and icing sugar in a jug or bottle, and then just filling glasses that already have the lemon slices, ice cubes and mint in them.

*Makes about 1.5 litres
(52 fl oz/6 cups)*

1 lemon
250 g (9 oz) strawberries, hulled
1 tablespoon icing
    (confectioners') sugar
150 ml (5 fl oz) cranberry juice
1.25 litres (44 fl oz/5 cups) chilled
    soda water (club soda)
ice cubes and mint leaves,
    to serve

Juice half the lemon, then cut the remaining half into thin slices.

In a blender, process the strawberries until smooth, then pour into a jug and add in the lemon juice, icing sugar and cranberry juice. Combine well, then add the soda water, ice cubes and mint leaves. Serve immediately.

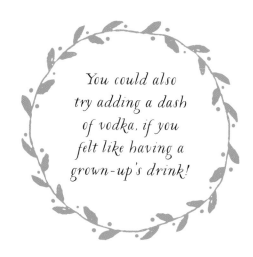

You could also try adding a dash of vodka, if you felt like having a grown-up's drink!

Strawberry, Mint & Ginger Syrup

Makes 1 litre
(35 fl oz/4 cups)

880 g (1 lb 15 oz/4 cups) sugar
250 g (9 oz) strawberries, hulled
    and chopped
1 large handful mint leaves, plus
    extra, to garnish
50 g (1¾ oz) fresh ginger, peeled
    and sliced
juice and grated zest of 2 lemons
250 ml (9 fl oz/1 cup) white
    balsamic vinegar
chilled water, soda water (club
    soda) or lemonade, to serve
lemon slices, to garnish

Put the sugar in a saucepan with 500 ml
(17 fl oz/2 cups) water and stir over low heat
until the sugar dissolves. Add the strawberries,
mint, ginger, lemon juice and zest. Bring to the
boil, then reduce the heat and simmer for
20 minutes.

Remove from the heat, stir in the vinegar, then
stand overnight to allow the flavours to infuse.
Strain, then pour the syrup into sterilised
bottles or jars (page 20) and seal.

To serve, combine one part syrup with five
parts chilled water, soda water or lemonade.
Garnish with mint leaves and lemon slices.

Once you've
opened a bottle of
syrup, keep any
unused portion in
the fridge.

Strawberry Nests

Sweet and refreshing with mint, this dessert is an oldie but a goodie. What's great is that you can have all the elements ready to go and just assemble it at the last minute for your guests. You could also try some basil instead of the mint, if you wanted to be adventurous.

Serves 4

2 tablespoons balsamic vinegar
185 ml (6 fl oz/¾ cup)
   non-alcoholic apple cider or
   clear apple juice
1 tablespoon honey
250 g (9 oz) strawberries, hulled
   and quartered
1 small handful mint leaves
1 teaspoon caster (superfine)
   sugar
4 meringue nests or cups
   (available from supermarkets)
thick (double) cream, to serve
   (optional)

Put the vinegar, apple cider and honey in a small saucepan and stir over low heat until reduced and syrupy, but not too thick. Remove from the heat and allow to cool.

Put the strawberries in a bowl with the mint and sugar and toss to combine.

Divide the strawberries among the meringue nests, drizzle each with a little balsamic glaze and serve immediately with cream (if using).

If you're in a hurry, use store-bought balsamic glaze or even pure balsamic vinegar, for drizzling.

Apple & Strawberry Crumble

Although this lovely old-fashioned dessert is best assembled just before baking, the fruit filling and the crumble topping can both be made in advance and frozen, separately, for up to three months.

Serves 4

110 g (3¾ oz/½ cup) sugar
grated zest of ½ lemon
8 granny smith apples, peeled,
    cored and chopped
250 g (9 oz) strawberries, hulled
    and halved

CRUMBLE TOPPING
120 g (4¼ oz) unsalted butter,
    chilled, chopped
75 g (2¾ oz/½ cup) plain
    (all-purpose) flour
45 g (1½ oz/¼ cup lightly packed)
    light brown sugar
25 g (1 oz/¼ cup) almond meal
25 g (1 oz) hazelnuts, toasted,
    peeled and chopped
50 g (1¾ oz) blanched almonds,
    toasted and chopped
25 g (1 oz/¼ cup) rolled oats
    (porridge oats)

Preheat the oven to 210°C (415°F).

For the crumble topping, put the butter, flour, sugar and almond meal in a bowl. Using your fingertips, rub the butter into the dry ingredients until the mixture resembles coarse breadcrumbs. Add the nuts and oats, combine well and refrigerate until needed.

For the filling, put the sugar, zest and 125 ml (4 fl oz/½ cup) water in a saucepan and stir over low heat until the sugar dissolves. Add the apples and simmer for 15 minutes, or until half-cooked.

Spoon the apple evenly into a 19 x 19 x 7 cm (7½ x 7½ x 2¾ inch) baking dish (or four individual 250 ml/9 fl oz/1 cup) ramekins), scatter with the strawberries and top with the crumble mixture. Bake for 20 minutes, or until golden.

Strawberry Tarts

Serves 6

300 ml (10½ fl oz) thickened
    (whipping) cream
1 tablespoon icing
    (confectioners') sugar
½ teaspoon vanilla bean paste
750 g (1 lb 10 oz) strawberries,
    hulled and sliced
mint leaves, to garnish

PASTRY
225 g (8 oz/1½ cups) plain
    (all-purpose) flour
pinch of salt
150 g (5½ oz) unsalted butter,
    chilled, chopped
85 g (3 oz/⅔ cup) icing
    (confectioners') sugar
2 teaspoons baking powder
3 egg yolks, lightly whisked

For the pastry, sift the flour and salt into a bowl. Using your fingertips, rub the butter into the flour until the mixture resembles coarse breadcrumbs. Stir in the icing sugar and baking powder, then add the egg yolks and combine until a dough forms. Shape the pastry into a disc, cover with plastic wrap and refrigerate for 30 minutes.

Preheat the oven to 180°C (350°F).

Roll out the dough on a lightly floured work surface until it is 5 mm (¼ inch) thick and use it to line the base and sides of six 6 x 11 x 2 cm (2½ x 4¼ x ¾ inch) rectangular loose-based fluted tart (flan) tins. Line the pastry cases with baking paper, fill with baking beads or raw rice and bake for 10 minutes, or until the edges are light golden.

Remove the paper and the baking beads or rice and bake for a further 10 minutes, or until golden and dry. Remove from the oven and cool.

To serve, whisk the cream, icing sugar and vanilla bean paste until soft peaks form. Spoon the cream over the cooled pastry, top with the strawberry slices and serve immediately.

Strawberry Jam

If you're growing the strawberries, it might seem that you need a lot to make this jam, but it is well worth it. Homemade jam has such a lovely dark colour and it tastes so much better than the store-bought versions. It will keep in the cupboard for up to a year and also makes a great gift.

Makes about 640 g
(1 lb 6½ oz / 2 cups)

225 g (8 oz) sugar
450 g (1 lb) strawberries, hulled
    and coarsely chopped
1 tablespoon lemon juice

Put the sugar and strawberries in a heavy-based saucepan and cook over medium heat for 15 minutes, or until the fruit is soft and the jam has reached setting point. To test whether the jam has reached its setting point, spoon a little onto a chilled saucer and place in the freezer for 5 minutes. Using your finger, draw a line through the jam and if the line holds, then the jam is set.

(The cooking time will vary depending on how ripe your strawberries are – the riper the fruit, the less time it will take to cook. Do not leave the jam unattended once cooking, as it can easily catch on the base of the pan and burn.)

Stir in the lemon juice, then spoon the hot jam into hot sterilised jars (page 20) and seal.

Once the jam is opened, it will keep for up to 3 months in the fridge.

Index

ACKNOWLEDGMENTS

I'd like to thank the team at Murdoch Books, to whom I am extremely grateful for everything they have done, especially Corinne Roberts for believing in me.
To Melissa Guiney and Catherine Gratez, for helping me with the cooking.
To all the special women in my life – my mum, grandmother and old friends – I have managed to include a little something from all of you. The strength and encouragement you share with me have helped me achieve this book.

Published in 2015 by Murdoch Books, an imprint of Allen & Unwin

Murdoch Books Australia
83 Alexander Street
Crows Nest NSW 2065
Phone: +61 (0) 2 8425 0100
Fax: +61 (0) 2 9906 2218
www.murdochbooks.com.au
info@murdochbooks.com.au

Murdoch Books UK
Erico House, 6th Floor
93–99 Upper Richmond Road
Putney, London SW15 2TG
Phone: +44 (0) 20 8785 5995
www.murdochbooks.co.uk
info@murdochbooks.co.uk

For Corporate Orders & Custom Publishing contact
Noel Hammond, National Business Development Manager, Murdoch Books Australia

Publisher: Corinne Roberts
Design Manager: Hugh Ford
Editorial Manager: Barbara McClenahan
Designer: Kristine Lindbjerg
Editor: Georgina Bitcon
Food Editor: Christine Osmond
Production Manager: Mary Bjelobrk

Text and photography © Natalie Boog 2015
The moral rights of the author have been asserted.
Design © Murdoch Books 2015

A cataloguing-in-publication entry is available from the catalogue of the National Library of Australia at www.nla.gov.au.

ISBN 978 1 76011 065 9 Australia
ISBN 978 1 74336 326 3 UK

A catalogue record for this book is available from the British Library.

Colour reproduction by Splitting Image Colour Studio Pty Ltd, Clayton, Victoria
Printed by Hang Tai Printing Company Limited, Hong Kong

IMPORTANT: Those who might be at risk from the effects of salmonella poisoning (the elderly, pregnant women, young children and those suffering from immune deficiency diseases) should consult their doctor with any concerns about eating raw eggs.

OVEN GUIDE: You may find cooking times vary depending on the oven you are using. For fan-forced ovens, as a general rule, set the oven temperature to 20°C (35°F) lower than indicated in the recipe.

MEASURES GUIDE: We have used 20 ml (4 teaspoon) tablespoon measures. If you are using a 15 ml (3 teaspoon) tablespoon add an extra teaspoon of the ingredient for each tablespoon specified.